Praise for the first edition of

The European Union: A Very Short Introduction

'John Pinder has for years been recognized and respected as an outstanding authority on European Community, now European Union affairs. This short, detailed yet splendidly readable book...is a must for anyone seeking to understand the European Union, its origins, development, and possible future.'

Michael Palliser

'John Pinder writes straightforwardly and beautifully clearly...He has done an extraordinary job of compressing the history and the book is absolutely up to date.'

Helen Wallace, Sussex European Institute

'John Pinder is in a class of his own. He brings clarity and vision to what is too often complicated and obscure. He causes both friend and foe to wonder what a reformed and strengthened Union could achieve for all Europe and for the wider world.'

Andrew Duff, MEP, Constitutional Affairs Spokesman, European Liberal Democrats

'...indispensable not only for beginners but for all interested in European issues. Pithy, lucid and accessible it covers recent history, institutions, and policies, as well as future developments.'
Rt. Hon. Giles Radice, MP

'it not only lives up to but exceeds the promise of its title. This is in fact "The European Union – A Very Short, Useful and Straightforward Guide".'

Independent on Sunday

'invaluable'

William Keegan, *Observer*

VERY SHORT INTRODUCTIONS are for anyone wanting a stimulating and accessible way in to a new subject. They are written by experts, and have been published in more than 25 languages worldwide.

The series began in 1995, and now represents a wide variety of topics in history, philosophy, religion, science, and the humanities. Over the next few years it will grow to a library of around 200 volumes – a Very Short Introduction to everything from ancient Egypt and Indian philosophy to conceptual art and cosmology.

Very Short Introductions available now:

AFRICAN HISTORY
    John Parker and Richard Rathbone
AMERICAN POLITICAL
    PARTIES AND ELECTIONS
    L. Sandy Maisel
THE AMERICAN
    PRESIDENCY Charles O. Jones
ANARCHISM Colin Ward
ANCIENT EGYPT Ian Shaw
ANCIENT PHILOSOPHY
    Julia Annas
ANCIENT WARFARE
    Harry Sidebottom
ANGLICANISM Mark Chapman
THE ANGLO-SAXON AGE
    John Blair
ANIMAL RIGHTS David DeGrazia
ANTISEMITISM Steven Beller
ARCHAEOLOGY Paul Bahn
ARCHITECTURE
    Andrew Ballantyne
ARISTOTLE Jonathan Barnes
ART HISTORY Dana Arnold
ART THEORY Cynthia Freeland

THE HISTORY OF
    ASTRONOMY Michael Hoskin
ATHEISM Julian Baggini
AUGUSTINE Henry Chadwick
BARTHES Jonathan Culler
BESTSELLERS John Sutherland
THE BIBLE John Riches
THE BRAIN Michael O'Shea
BRITISH POLITICS
    Anthony Wright
BUDDHA Michael Carrithers
BUDDHISM Damien Keown
BUDDHIST ETHICS
    Damien Keown
CAPITALISM James Fulcher
THE CELTS Barry Cunliffe
CHAOS Leonard Smith
CHOICE THEORY
    Michael Allingham
CHRISTIAN ART
    Beth Williamson
CHRISTIANITY Linda Woodhead
CLASSICS Mary Beard and
    John Henderson

Available soon:

For more information visit our website

www.oup.co.uk/general/vsi/

John Pinder and
Simon Usherwood

THE EUROPEAN
UNION

A Very Short Introduction

OXFORD
UNIVERSITY PRESS

Great Clarendon Street, Oxford OX2 6DP

Oxford University Press is a department of the University of Oxford.
It furthers the University's objective of excellence in research, scholarship,
and education by publishing worldwide in

Oxford New York

Auckland Cape Town Dar es Salaam Hong Kong Karachi
Kuala Lumpur Madrid Melbourne Mexico City Nairobi
New Delhi Shanghai Taipei Toronto

With offices in

Argentina Austria Brazil Chile Czech Republic France Greece
Guatemala Hungary Italy Japan Poland Portugal Singapore
South Korea Switzerland Thailand Turkey Ukraine Vietnam

Oxford is a registered trade mark of Oxford University Press
in the UK and in certain other countries

Published in the United States
by Oxford University Press Inc., New York

British Library Cataloguing in Publication Data

Data available

Library of Congress Cataloging in Publication Data

Data available

ISBN 978-0-19-923397-7

5 7 9 10 8 6 4

Typeset by SPI Publisher Services, Pondicherry, India
Printed in Great Britain by
Ashford Colour Press Ltd, Gosport, Hampshire

Contents

Foreword

Some say it was Shaw who apologized for writing a long letter because he hadn't time to write a short one, some say Voltaire. Doubtless both did. They might have said the same about writing this book. Brevity is a tough constraint when the need is to explain succinctly such a complex entity as the European Union.

The core of the problem is to concentrate on the essentials. John, who was the sole author of the first edition, has been following the development of the Community, now the Union, since its inception over half a century ago, and acquired a large stock of facts and ideas from which to choose what seem to be the most relevant for this book. He soon formed the view that it would be best to move by steps and stages in a federal direction and has seen no reason to change it. This does not mean pulling up the old nations of Europe by the roots and trying to plant them in virgin soil, but developing a framework in which they can deal with their common problems in an effective and democratic way. His choice of ideas is inevitably coloured by this view. While Simon's view is not identical, there is nothing in it with which he is not at ease.

The concern of both of us has been to present the ideas in a way that will help to provide a context for reasonable people, whether they lean towards a federal or an intergovernmental approach, to evaluate the performance of the Union and judge in which direction it should go. And we have endeavoured to be scrupulous about the facts.

Developments in the Union since the first edition was completed, nearly seven years ago, have been so extensive that we have agreed to share the work on this one. John has revised his chapters 1, 2, 3, 8, and 11; Simon has revised chapters 4, 5, 6, 7, and 9; and both have worked on chapter 10. Simon has provided the boxes, charts, chronology, glossary, and maps. Special thanks are due to Iain Begg, Andrew Duff, Nigel Haigh, Christopher Johnson, Jörg Monar, and Simon Nuttall; while those responsible at OUP combined efficiency with understanding of authors' needs. If what follows does not please the reader, it is no fault of theirs.

May 2007

John Pinder
Simon Usherwood

Abbreviations

ACP	African, Caribbean, Pacific countries
AFSJ	Area of Freedom, Security and Justice
Benelux	Belgium, Netherlands, and Luxembourg
CAP	common agricultural policy
CFC	chlorofluorocarbon
CFSP	Common Foreign and Security Policy
CIS	Commonwealth of Independent States
CJHA	Cooperation in Justice and Home Affairs
CO_2	carbon dioxide
Comecon	Council for Mutual Economic Assistance
Coreper	Committee of Permanent Representatives
EAGGF	European Agricultural Guidance and Guarantee Fund
EC	European Community
ECB	European Central Bank
ECJ	European Court of Justice (formal title, Court of Justice)
Ecofin	Council of Economic and Finance Ministers
Ecosoc	Economic and Social Committee
ECSC	European Coal and Steel Community
ecu	European Currency Unit (forerunner of euro)
EDC	European Defence Community
EDF	European Development Fund
EEC	European Economic Community
EEA	European Economic Area
Efta	European Free Trade Association
EMS	European Monetary System
Emu	Economic and Monetary Union

ENP	European Neighbourhood Policy
EPC	European Political Cooperation
ERDF	European Regional Development Fund
ERM	Exchange Rate Mechanism
ESCB	European System of Central Banks
ESDP	European Security and Defence Policy
ESF	European Social Fund
EU	European Union
Euratom	European Atomic Energy Community
Gatt	General Agreement on Tariffs and Trade (forerunner of WTO)
GDP	Gross Domestic Product
GNP	Gross National Product
GSP	Generalized System of Preferences
IGC	Intergovernmental Conference
Nato	North Atlantic Treaty Organization
NTBs	non-tariff barriers
OECD	Organization for Economic Cooperation and Development
OMC	Open method of coordination
OSCE	Organization for Security and Cooperation in Europe
PHARE	Poland and Hungary: aid for economic reconstruction (extended to other Central and East European countries)
QMV	qualified majority voting (in the Council)
SEA	Single European Act
TACIS	Technical Assistance to the CIS
TEC	Treaty establishing the European Community
TEU	Treaty on European Union
UN	United Nations
VAT	value-added tax
WEU	Western European Union
WTO	World Trade Organization

List of boxes

List of charts

List of illustrations

List of maps

Chapter 1
What the EU is for

The European Union of today is the result of a process that began over half a century ago with the creation of the European Coal and Steel Community. Those two industries then still provided the industrial muscle for military power; and Robert Schuman, the French Foreign Minister, affirmed on 9 May 1950 in his declaration which launched the project that 'any war between France and Germany' would become 'not merely unthinkable, but materially impossible'.

A durable peace

It may not be easy, at today's distance, to appreciate how much this meant, only five years after the end of the war of 1939–45 that had brought such terrible suffering to almost all European countries. For France and Germany, which had been at war with each other three times in the preceding eight decades, finding a way to live together in a durable peace was a fundamental political priority that the new Community was designed to serve.

For France the prospect of a completely independent Germany, with its formidable industrial potential, was alarming. The attempt to keep Germany down, as the French had tried to do after the 1914–18 war, had failed disastrously. The idea of binding

Germany within strong institutions, which would equally bind France and other European countries and thus be acceptable to Germans over the longer term, seemed more promising. That promise has been amply fulfilled. The French could regard the European Community (EC) and now the European Union (EU) as the outcome of their original initiative, and they sought, with considerable success, to play the part of a leader among European nations, though since the accession of 12 new member states in 2005 and 2007, they have become less confident of their leadership role.

But participation in these European institutions on an equal basis has also given Germany a framework within which to develop peaceful and constructive relations with the growing number of other member states, as well as to complete their unification smoothly in 1990. Following the 12 years of Nazi rule that ended with devastation in 1945, the Community offered Germans a way to become a respected people again. The idea of a Community of equals with strong institutions was attractive. Schuman had also declared that the new Community would be 'the first concrete foundation of a European federation which is indispensable to the preservation of peace'. But whereas French commitment to developing the Community in a federal direction has been variable, the German political class, having thoroughly absorbed the concept of federal democracy, has quite consistently supported such development. In 1992, indeed, an amendment to the Basic Law of the reunited Germany provided for its participation in the European Union committed to federal principles.

The other four founder states, Belgium, Italy, Luxembourg, and the Netherlands, also saw the new Community as a means to ensure peace by binding Germany within strong European institutions. For the most part they too, like the Germans, saw the Community as a stage in the development of a federal polity and have largely continued to do so.

2

Although World War Two is receding into a more distant past, the motive of peace and security within a democratic polity that was fundamental to the foundation of the Community remains a powerful influence on governments and politicians in many of the member states. The system that has provided a framework for over half a century of peace is regarded as a guarantee of future stability. A recent example was the decision to consolidate it by introducing the single currency, seen as a way to reinforce the safe anchorage of the potentially more powerful Germany after its unification; the accession of ten Central and East European states, seeking a safe haven after the Second World War followed by half a century of Soviet domination, was another; and there has been continuing pressure to strengthen the Union's institutions in order to maintain stability as eastern enlargement increases the number of member states towards 30 or more, including several new democracies.

The British, having avoided the experience of defeat and occupation, did not share that fundamental motive for the sharing of sovereignty with other European peoples and felt reliance on the US and Nato to be sufficient. Hence the focus on the economic aspects of integration that has been common among British politicians and has restricted their ability to play an influential and constructive part in some of the most significant developments. The EU's potential contribution to making the world a safer place in fields such as climate change and peacekeeping, as well as with its external economic and aid policies more generally, could, however, as suggested later in this book, provide grounds for a change in this fundamental British attitude.

Economic strength and prosperity

While a durable peace was a profound political motive for establishing the new Community, it would not have succeeded without adequate performance in the economic field in which it was given its powers; and the Community did in fact serve economic as well as political logic. The frontiers between France, Germany, Belgium, and Luxembourg, standing between steel plants and the mines whose coal they required, impeded rational production; and the removal of those barriers, accompanied by common governance of the resulting common market, was successful in economic terms. This, together with the evidence that peaceful reconciliation among the member states was being achieved, encouraged them to see the European Coal and Steel Community as a first step, as Schuman had indicated, in a process of political as well as economic unification. After an unsuccessful attempt at a second step, when the French National Assembly failed to ratify a treaty for a European Defence Community in 1954, the six founder states proceeded again on the path of economic integration. The concept of the common market was extended to the whole of their mutual trade in goods when the European Economic Community (EEC) was founded in 1958, opening up the way to an integrated economy that responded to the logic of economic interdependence among the member states.

The EEC was also, thanks to French insistence on surrounding the common market with a common external tariff, able to enter trade negotiations on level terms with the United States; and this demonstrated the potential of the Community to become a major actor in the international system when it has a common instrument with which to conduct an external policy. It was a first step towards satisfying another motive for creating the Community: to restore European influence in the wider world, which had been dissipated by the two great fratricidal wars, and which can now be reinforced by the Union's potential for contributing to much-needed global safety and prosperity.

One exception to the British failure to understand the strength of the case for such radical reform was Winston Churchill who, less than a year and a half after the end of the war, said in a

1. **Churchill at The Hague: founds the European Movement, following his call for 'a kind of United States of Europe'**

speech in Zurich: 'We must now build a kind of United States of Europe ... the first step must be a partnership between France and Germany ... France and Germany must take the lead together.' But few among the British understood so well the case for a new Community, and Churchill himself did not feel that Britain, then at the head of its Empire and with a recently forged special relationship with the United States, should be a member. Many were, however, reluctant to be disadvantaged in Continental markets and excluded from the taking of important policy decisions. So after failing to secure a free trade area that would incorporate the EEC as well as other West European countries, successive British governments sought entry into the Community, finally succeeding in 1973. But while the British played a leading part in developing the common market into a more complete single market, they continued to lack the political motives that have driven the founder states, as well as some others, to press towards other forms of deeper integration.

It is important to understand the motives of the founders and of the British which, while they continue to evolve, still influence attitudes towards the European Union. Such motives are shared, in various proportions, by other states which have acceded over the years; and they underlie much of the drama that has unfolded since 1950 to produce the Union which is the subject of this book.

Theories and explanations

There are two main ways of explaining the phenomenon of the Community and the Union. Adherents to one emphasize the role of the member states and their intergovernmental dealings; adherents to the other give greater weight to the European institutions.

Most of the former, belonging to the 'realist' or 'neo-realist' schools of thought, hold that the Community and the Union have not wrought any fundamental change in the relationships among the member states, whose governments continue to pursue their national interests and seek to maximize their power within the EU as elsewhere. A more recent variant, called liberal intergovernmentalism, looks to the play of forces in their domestic politics to explain the governments' behaviour in the Union. For want of a better word, 'intergovernmentalist' is used below for this family of explanations as to how the Community and Union work.

One should not underestimate the role that the governments retain in the Union's affairs, with their power of decision in the Council that represents the member states and their monopoly of the *ultima ratio* of armed force. But other approaches, including those known as neo-functionalism and federalism, give more weight than the intergovernmentalists to the European institutions.

Neo-functionalists saw the Community developing by a process of 'spillover' from the original ECSC, with its scope confined to only two industrial sectors. Interest groups and political parties, attracted by the success of the Community in dealing with the problems of these two sectors, would become frustrated by its inability to deal with related problems in other fields and would, with leadership from the European Commission, press successfully for the Community's competence to be extended, until it would eventually provide a form of European governance for a wide range of the affairs of the member states. This offers at least a partial explanation of some steps in the Community's development, including the move from the single market to the single currency.

A federalist perspective, while also stressing the importance of the common institutions, goes beyond neo-functionalism in two main ways. First, it relates the transfer of powers to the Union less to a spillover from existing powers to new ones than to the growing inability of governments to deal effectively with problems that have become transnational and so escape the reach of existing states. Most of these problems concern the economy, the environment, and security; and the states should retain control over matters with which they can still cope adequately. Second, whereas neo-functionalists have not been clear about the principles that would shape the European institutions, a federalist perspective is based on principles of liberal democracy: in particular, the rule of law based on fundamental rights, and representative government with the laws enacted and the executive controlled by elected representatives of the citizens. In this view, the powers exercised jointly need to be dealt with by institutions of government, because the intergovernmental method is neither effective nor democratic enough to satisfy the needs of citizens of democratic states. So either the federal elements in the institutions will be strengthened until the Union becomes an effective democratic polity, based on the principles of rule of law and representative government; or it will fail to attract enough support from the citizens to enable it to flourish, and perhaps even to survive.

Subsequent chapters will try to show how far the development of the Community and the Union has reflected these different views. Meanwhile the reader should be warned: the authors consider that the need for effective and democratic government has moved the EC and the EU by steps and stages quite far in a federal direction and should, but by no means certainly will, continue to do so.

Chapter 2
How the EU was made

'Europe will not be made all at once, or according to a single, general plan. It will be built through concrete achievements, which first create a de facto solidarity.' With these words, the Schuman declaration accurately predicted the way in which the Community has become the Union of today. The institutions and powers have been developed step by step, following the confidence gained through the success of preceding steps, to deal with matters that appeared to be best handled by common action.

Subsequent chapters consider particular institutions and fields of competence in more detail. Here we see how interests and events combined to bring about the development as a whole. Some primary interests and motives were considered in the previous chapter: security, not just through military means but by establishing economic and political relationships; prosperity, with business and trade unions particularly interested; protection of the environment, with pressure from green parties and voluntary organizations, and with climate change a matter of increasingly general concern; and influence in external relations, to promote common interests in the wider world.

With the creation of the Community to serve such purposes, other interests came into play. Those who feared damage from certain aspects sought compensation through redistributive measures:

for France, the common agricultural policy to counterbalance German industrial advantage; the structural funds for countries with weaker economies, which feared they would lose from the single market; budgetary adjustments for the British and others with high net contributions. Some governments, parliaments, parties, and voluntary organizations have pressed for reforms aiming to make the institutions more effective and democratic. Against them have stood those who resist moves beyond intergovernmental decision-making, acting from a variety of motives: ideological commitment to the nation-state; a belief that democracy is feasible only within and not beyond it; mistrust of foreigners; and simple attachment to the status quo. Among them have been such historic figures as President de Gaulle and Prime Minister Thatcher, as well as a wide range of institutions and individuals, most prevalent among the British, Danes, Czechs, and Poles. Among the European institutions, it is the Council of Ministers that has come closest to this view.

Two of the most influential federalists, committed to the development of a European polity that would deal effectively with the common interests of the member states and their citizens, have been Jean Monnet and Jacques Delors. Both initiated major steps towards a federal aim. Altiero Spinelli represented a different kind of federalism, envisaging more radical moves towards a European constitution. The German, Italian, Belgian, and Dutch parliaments and governments have in varying degrees been institutionally federalist, as have the European Commission and Parliament, and, in so far as the treaties could be interpreted in that way, the Court of Justice. They have generally preferred Monnet's stepwise approach, although the Belgians, Italians, and European Parliament have espoused constitutional federalism.

1950s: the founding treaties

Monnet was responsible for drafting the Schuman declaration, chaired the negotiations for the ECSC Treaty, and was the first

President of its High Authority. These two words reflected his insistence on a strong executive at the centre of the Community, stemming originally from his experience as Deputy Secretary General of the interwar League of Nations which convinced him of the weakness of an intergovernmental system. He was, however, persuaded that, for democratic member states, such a Community should be provided with a parliamentary assembly and a court – embryonic elements of a federal legislature and judiciary – and that there should be a council of ministers of the member states.

This structure has remained remarkably stable to this day, though the relationship between the institutions has changed: the Council, and in particular, since 1974, the European Council of government heads, has become the most powerful; the European Commission, while still very important, has lost ground to it;

2. Monnet (left) and Schuman (right)

Le 6 Mai 1950

La paix mondiale ne saurait être sauvegardée sans des efforts créateurs à la mesure des dangers qui la menacent.

La contribution qu'une Europe organisée et vivante peut apporter à la civilisation est indispensable au maintien des relations pacifiques. En se faisant depuis plus de 20 ans le champion d'une Europe unie, la France a toujours eu pour objet essentiel de servir la paix. L'Europe n'a pas été faite, nous avons eu la guerre.

L'Europe ne se fera pas d'un coup, ni dans une construction d'ensemble : elle se fera par des réalisations concrètes créant d'abord une solidarité de fait. Le rassemblement des nations européennes exige que l'opposition séculaire de la France et de l'Allemagne soit éliminée : l'action entreprise doit toucher au premier chef la France et l'Allemagne.

Dans ce but, le Gouvernement Français propose de porter immédiatement l'action sur un point limité mais décisif :

Le Gouvernement Français propose de placer l'ensemble de la production franco-allemande de charbon et d'acier, sous une Haute Autorité commune, dans une organisation ouverte à la participation des autres pays d'Europe.

La mise en commun des productions de charbon et d'acier assurera immédiatement l'établissement de bases communes de développement économique, première étape de la Fédération européenne, et changera le destin de ces régions longtemps vouées à la fabrication des armes de guerre dont elles ont été les plus constantes victimes.

3. Page one of the text Monnet sent to Schuman for his Declaration of 9 May 1950

the European Parliament has gained in power; and the Court of Justice has established itself as the supreme judicial authority in matters of Community competence. Although they were later to accept these institutions, British governments of the 1950s felt them to be too federal for British participation.

The six member states, however, were minded to proceed further in that direction. The French government reacted to American insistence on German rearmament, following the impact of communist expansionism in both Europe and Korea, by proposing a European Defence Community with a European army. An EDC Treaty was signed by the six governments and ratified by four; but opposition grew in France and the Assemblée Nationale voted in 1954 to shelve it. The result was that the idea of a competence in the field of defence remained a no-go area until the 1990s.

While the collapse of the EDC was a severe setback, confidence in the Community as a framework for peaceful relations among the member states had grown; and there was a powerful political impulse to 'relaunch' its development. The Dutch were ready with a proposal for a general common market, for which the support of Belgium and Germany was soon forthcoming. The French, still markedly protectionist, were doubtful. But they held to the project of European unification built around Franco-German partnership and so accepted the common market which the Germans wanted, on condition that other French interests were satisfied: an atomic energy community in which France was equipped to play the leading part; the common agricultural policy; the association of colonial territories on favourable terms; and equal pay for women throughout the Community, without which French industry, already required by French law to pay it, would in some sectors have been at a competitive disadvantage. The Italians for their part, who had the weakest economy among the six, secured the European Investment Bank, the Social Fund, and free movement of labour. So all these elements were included in the two Rome Treaties, which established the European Economic Community (EEC) and European Atomic Energy Community (Euratom): an early example of a package deal, incorporating advantages for each member state, which has characterized many of the steps taken since then.

The Treaties

Rome wasn't built in a day; and the Treaties of Rome (in force in 1958) were a big building block in a long and complicated process that has constructed the present European Union. Other major treaties included the ECSC Treaty (in force 1952), Single European Act (1987), Maastricht (1993), Amsterdam Treaty (1999), Nice Treaty (2002).

A minor complication is that there were two Treaties of Rome (see below), but the EEC Treaty was so much more important than the Euratom Treaty that it is generally known as *the* Treaty of Rome.

A major complication is that the European Union was set up by the Maastricht Treaty, with two new 'pillars' for foreign policy and internal security alongside the European Community, which already had its own treaties. These have been consolidated in the EC Treaty (TEC), which continues to exist alongside the EU Treaty (TEU) though the EC is an integral part of the EU. So there are now two Treaties, closely linked and with common institutions, though the Court of Justice, the Commission, and the European Parliament play a more important role in the EC than in the other two pillars.

N.B. to avoid undue complexity, this book follows two principles in referring to the EC and EU:

- European Community, Community, or EC is used regarding matters relating entirely to the time before the EU was established, or after that time if the EC's separate characteristics are relevant;
- European, Union, or EU in all other cases.

The two new treaties entered into force on 1 January 1958. Euratom was sidelined by de Gaulle, who became President of France in the middle of that year and was determined to keep the French atomic sector national, in the service of French military power. But the EEC became the basis for the future development of the Community. Its institutions were similar to those of the ECSC, though with a somewhat less powerful executive, called Commission instead of High Authority; and the EEC was given a wide range of economic competences, including the power to establish a customs union with internal free trade and a common external tariff; policies for particular sectors, notably agriculture; and more general cooperation.

The first President of the Commission, Walter Hallstein, was a very able former professor of law and convinced federalist who, as a senior figure in Chancellor Adenauer's government, had been

4. De Gaulle says 'non' to Britain

5. Thatcher says 'no' to the single currency

Monnet's principal partner in negotiating the ECSC Treaty. He led the Commission into a flying start, with acceleration of the timetable for establishing the customs union; and within this framework the Community enjoyed notable economic success in the 1960s, with growth averaging some 5% a year, twice as fast as in Britain and the United States. But conflict between the emergent federal Community, as conceived by Monnet or Hallstein, and de Gaulle's fundamentalist commitment to the nation-state made that decade politically hazardous for the Community.

The 1960s: de Gaulle against the federalists

In June 1958, less than six months after the Rome Treaties came into force, de Gaulle became French President. He did not like the federal elements and aspirations of the Community. But nor was he prepared to challenge directly treaties recently ratified by France. He sought, rather, to use the Community as a means to advance French power and leadership. One example was his sidelining of Euratom. Another was his veto which terminated in 1963 the first negotiations to enlarge the Community to include Britain, Denmark, Ireland, and Norway. Although the British government's conception of the Community was closer to that of de Gaulle than of the other, more federalist-minded member states' governments, and Britain's defence of its agricultural and Commonwealth interests had irked them by making the negotiations hard and long, they resented the unilateral and nationalist manner of the veto so deeply that it provoked the first political crisis within the Community. This was followed, in 1965, by a greater crisis over the arrangements for the common agricultural policy (CAP).

The CAP had from the outset been a key French interest and de Gaulle was determined to have it established without undue delay. It was to be based on price supports requiring substantial public expenditure. Both France and the Commission agreed that this should come from the budget of the Community, not the member states. But the Commission, with its federalist orientation, and the Dutch parliament, with its deep commitment to democratic principles, insisted that the budget spending must be subject to parliamentary control; and since a European budget could not be controlled by six separate parliaments, it would have to be done by the European Parliament. This suited the other governments well enough, but was anathema to de Gaulle. He precipitated the crisis of 'the empty chair', forbidding his ministers to attend meetings of the Council throughout the second half of 1965 and evoking fears among the other states that he might be preparing to destroy the Community.

Neither side was willing to give way and the episode concluded in January 1966 with the so-called 'Luxembourg compromise'.

The French government asserted a right of veto when interests 'very important to one or more member states' are at stake; and the other five affirmed their commitment to the treaty provision for qualified majority voting on certain questions, which was that very month due to come into effect for votes on a wide range of subjects. In practice de Gaulle's view prevailed for the next two decades, so that Luxembourg 'veto' seems a more accurate description than 'compromise'. In the mid-1980s, however, majority voting began to be practised in the context of the single market programme, and has now become the standard procedure applicable to most legislative decisions.

Despite these conflicts between the intergovernmental and the federal conceptions, the customs union was completed by July 1968, earlier than the treaty required. Its impact had already been felt not only internally but also in the Community's external relations. Wielding the common instrument of the external tariff, the Community was becoming, in the field of trade, a power comparable to the United States. President Kennedy had reacted by proposing multilateral negotiations for major tariff cuts. Skilfully led by the Commission, the Community responded positively; and the outcome was cuts averaging one-third, initiating an era in which it was to become the major force for international trade liberalization.

Alongside the ups and downs of Community politics, the Court of Justice made steady progress in establishing the rule of law. Based on its treaty obligation to ensure that 'the law is observed', in judgments in 1963 and 1964 the Court established the principles of the primacy and the direct effect of Community law, so that it would be consistently applied in all the member states. Though without the means of enforcement proper to a state, respect for the law, based on the treaties and on legislation enacted by its institutions, provided cement that has bound the Community together.

Widening and some deepening: Britain, Denmark, Ireland join

President de Gaulle resigned in 1969 and was replaced by Georges Pompidou. Nationalist fundamentalism as a basis for French policy gave way to pragmatic intergovernmentalism. Britain, Denmark, Ireland, and Norway still sought entry; France's partners supported it; and, instead of vetoing enlargement as de Gaulle had done, Pompidou consented, providing it was accompanied by conditions of interest to France: agreement on the financing of the CAP, as well as elements of 'deepening' such as monetary union and coordination of foreign policy. In addition to serving the French agricultural interest, these were intended to integrate Germany yet more firmly into the Community, as well as guard against the danger that widening the Community would weaken it.

France's partners favoured both widening and deepening. Germany's new Chancellor, the federalist Willy Brandt, played a leading part in a summit meeting of the six government heads in The Hague in December 1969. While he became famous for his Ostpolitik, relaxing tension with the Soviet bloc and with East Germany in particular, Brandt accompanied it with a Westpolitik for strengthening integration in the West. At The Hague he both promoted enlargement and proposed an economic and monetary union. This was agreed in principle, along with the other French conditions; and these projects were developed within the Community alongside the entry negotiations.

The principle of economic and monetary union was not, however, realized in practice until the 1990s. France, showing a preference for federal policy instruments rather than institutional reform, wanted a single currency. For Germany, this would have to be accompanied by coordination of economic policies, together with majority voting in the Council and powers for the European Parliament. But these were reforms too far for France in that early post-gaullist period. The result was a system for cooperation on exchange rates that was too weak to survive the international currency turbulence of that period. The system devised for foreign policy cooperation, kept separate from the Community owing to French insistence on sovereignty in this field, was strictly intergovernmental. Though quite useful, its impact was limited. It was the hard financial interest of French agriculture that secured a solid outcome, in a financial regulation that was to be highly disadvantageous for the British, whose small but efficient farm sector differed from those of the six member states.

The financing of the CAP again raised the question of powers for the European Parliament, on which the Dutch, supported by Belgium, Germany, and Italy, continued to insist. Pompidou's reaction was to accept the principle that the European Parliament would share control of the budget with the Council, but to exclude as much as possible of the expenditure, including in particular that on agriculture. This was accepted, faute de mieux, by France's partners in an amending treaty in 1970; and the Parliament's role was enhanced in a second treaty in 1975, after Pompidou had been succeeded by the post-gaullist President Giscard d'Estaing. While this was just a foot in the door to budgetary powers for the Parliament, it was to grow into a major element in the Community's institutional structure.

Though agriculture and Commonwealth trade still presented difficulties and the British public appeared unconvinced, Prime Minister Heath established good relations with President Pompidou and drove the entry negotiations through to a successful conclusion. Britain, together with Denmark and Ireland, joined the Community in January 1973, though the Norwegians rejected accession in a referendum. The British too were to vote in a referendum in 1975. Harold Wilson had replaced Edward Heath as Prime Minister in 1974 following an election victory by the Labour Party, which was turning more

6. British entry: Heath signs the Treaty of Accession

and more against the Community. After a somewhat cosmetic 'renegotiation', the Wilson government did recommend continued membership; and in 1975 the voters approved it by a two-to-one majority. But Labour became increasingly hostile, to the point of campaigning in the 1983 elections for British withdrawal. Meanwhile Margaret Thatcher had become Prime Minister as a result of the Conservative election victory in 1979. While French post-gaullist governments were moving back towards support for earlier concepts of the Community, she was developing a stormy relationship with it, fighting to assert the principle of intergovernmentalism. Until 1984 she also fought to 'get our money back', as she put it, by blocking much Community business until she secured agreement to reduce Britain's high net contribution to the Community's budget.

In 1974 President Pompidou died and Valéry Giscard d'Estaing succeeded him. Although Giscard had been de Gaulle's Finance Minister, he was not of the gaullist tradition and wanted to mark his presidency with measures to develop the Community. Ambivalent about federalism, he acted to strengthen both the intergovernmental and the federal elements in the Community's institutions, with initiatives to convert the summits into regular meetings, as the European Council of Heads of State and Government, as well as to launch direct elections to the European Parliament.

Following consultation with Monnet, who had remained active until then as President of the Action Committee for the United States of Europe in which he had brought together the leaders of the democratic political parties and trade unions of the member states, Giscard successfully proposed both the European Council and the direct elections. The European Council was soon to play a central part in taking Community decisions, settling conflicts that ministers in the Council were unable to resolve, and agreeing on major package deals. Provision had already been made for direct elections in the treaties of the 1950s, subject to unanimous agreement in the Council, which had been unattainable while gaullists ruled France. But the governments now agreed and the first elections were held in June 1979. This step towards representative democracy was to have a big impact on the Community's future development.

That year of the first direct elections also saw a significant move towards monetary union. On becoming President of the Commission in 1977, Roy Jenkins, formerly a leading member of the Labour government, who without being explicitly federalist favoured steps in a federal direction, had looked for a way to 'move Europe forward' and concluded that the time was ripe to revive the idea of monetary union. This was taken up by the German Chancellor, Helmut Schmidt, who saw it as a way to spread the burden of a difficult relationship with the US that resulted from the weakness of the dollar and the strength of the mark, and who was also influenced by Monnet's ideas. Schmidt and Giscard had forged a close relationship as Finance Ministers before becoming Chancellor and President in 1974; and they readily agreed on a proposal for a European Monetary System (EMS), with a strong mechanism for mutual exchange rate stability, and a European Currency Unit (ecu) to perform some technical functions. This was accepted by all save the British government, in the context of the Labour Party's growing hostility to the Community. So all but one of the member states participated in the EMS when it was created in 1979, alongside the Community rather than within it: an example of a recurrent pattern, with a number of states proceeding together while Britain, sometimes with one or two others, stands aside – usually deciding eventually to participate.

Single market, Draft Treaty on European Union, southern enlargement

Jacques Delors became President of the Commission in January 1985. He had visited each member state to find out what major project was likely to be accepted by all of them. As a federalist in Monnet's tradition, his short-list contained projects – single market, single currency, common defence policy, institutional reform – that could be seen as steps in a federal direction. But Thatcher, whose view of federalism was akin to de Gaulle's, and so was hostile to the currency, defence, and institutional projects, was at the same time a militant economic liberal who saw the single market as an important measure of trade liberalization. European economies had lost momentum during the hard times of the 1970s and all the governments accepted the single market project as a way to break out of what was then called eurosclerosis. The project was strongly backed by the more dynamic firms and the main business associations.

The common market as conceived by the EEC Treaty was in effect a single internal market. But while the treaty had specified the

7. **Delors: single market, single currency, single-minded European**

programme for abolishing tariffs and quotas, which had thus been successfully accomplished, it had provided for unanimous voting in the Council on most of the legislation required to remove non-tariff barriers; and the effect of the Luxembourg 'compromise' had been to apply this veto under another name to the rest. The result was scant progress towards their removal, while a resurgence of protectionist pressures during the 1970s, combined with the increasing complexity of the modern economy, had made them a severe impediment to trade.

The successful abolition of tariffs on internal trade had demonstrated the value of a programme with a timetable. So the Commission produced a list of some 300 measures to be enacted by the end of 1992 in order to complete the single market by removing the non-tariff barriers. The Commissioner in charge of the project was Lord Cockfield, a former minister in the Thatcher government; and the programme was rapidly drafted in time to be presented to the European Council in Milan in June 1985.

Meanwhile the European Parliament had prepared a political project: a Draft Treaty on European Union, inspired by Altiero Spinelli, the leading figure among those federalists who saw the drafting of a constitution as the royal road to federation. He had pursued this idea since the 1950s and now saw the directly elected Members of the European Parliament (MEPs), of whom he was one, as qualified to draft it. He inspired fellow MEPs to support the project, led the process of drafting, and the Parliament approved the result by a big majority of votes.

The Draft Treaty was designed to reform the Community's institutions so as to give them a federal character; to extend its powers to include most of those that would be normal in a federation, with the key exception of defence; and to come into effect when ratified by a majority of the member states containing at least two-thirds of the Community's population, with suitable arrangements to be negotiated with any states that did not ratify. While there was widespread support for the draft in most of the founder states, the German government was among those that were not prepared to countenance the probable exclusion of Britain. President Mitterrand did, however, express support for the draft, albeit in somewhat equivocal terms; and its main proposals were presented to the European Council in Milan along with the Commission's single market project.

The European Council decided to convene an Intergovernmental Conference (IGC) on treaty amendment, overriding British, Danish, and Greek opposition with its first-ever use of a majority vote. The IGC considered amendments relating not only to the single market programme but also to a number of the proposals in the Parliament's Draft Treaty. The outcome

8. Spinelli voting for his Draft Treaty on European Union

was the Single European Act, which provided for completion of
the single market by 1992; gave the Community competences
in the fields of the environment, technological research and
development, social policies relating to employment, and
'cohesion'; and brought the foreign policy cooperation into the
scope of the EEC Treaty – hence the title Single European Act,
to distinguish it from a proposal to keep foreign policy separate.
The Single Act also provided for qualified majority voting in a
number of areas of single market legislation, and strengthened
the European Parliament through a 'cooperation procedure'
which gave it influence over such legislation, together with a
procedure requiring its assent to treaties of association and
accession.

The Community was enlarged in 1981 to include Greece and, in 1986, Portugal and Spain. All three had been ruled by authoritarian regimes and saw the Community as a support for their democracies as well as for economic modernization. The Community for its part wanted them to be viable member states and to be supportive of its projects, such as the single market. It was to this end that the cohesion policy, based on a doubling of the structural funds for assisting the development of economically weaker regions, was included in the Single Act.

Thus the Single Act strengthened both the Community's powers and its institutions, with influence from a combination of governments, economic interests, social concerns, the Commission, the Parliament, and a variety of federalist forces. It was succeeded by the Maastricht, Amsterdam, and Nice Treaties, likewise strengthening both powers and institutions, and responding to similar combinations of pressures. This would not have happened had the Single Act not been successful. But the prospect of the single market helped to revive the economy, and the Community institutions gained in strength as they dealt with the vast programme of legislation.

Spinelli died a few weeks after the signing of the Single Act under the impression that it was a failure: 'a dead mouse', as he put it. In fact it initiated a relaunching of the Community which may have been as far-reaching in its effects as that which led to the Treaties of Rome.

Maastricht and Amsterdam Treaties, enlargement from 12 to 15

Following his success with the single market, Delors was determined to pursue the project of the single currency. Thatcher had not been alone in opposing it. Most Germans, proud of the deutschmark as the Community's strongest currency, were decidedly unenthusiastic. But it remained a major French

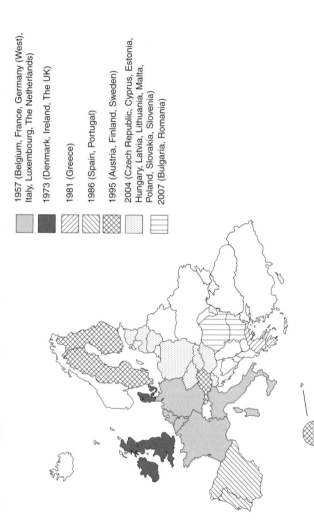

1957 (Belgium, France, Germany (West),
Italy, Luxembourg, The Netherlands)

1973 (Denmark, Ireland, The UK)

1981 (Greece)

1986 (Spain, Portugal)

1995 (Austria, Finland, Sweden)

2004 (Czech Republic, Cyprus, Estonia,
Hungary, Latvia, Lithuania, Malta,
Poland, Slovakia, Slovenia)

2007 (Bulgaria, Romania)

Map 1 Growth of the EU, 1957–2007

objective, for economic as well as political reasons; and Helmut Kohl, a long-standing federalist, held that it would be a crucial step towards a federal Europe. While he facilitated the preparation of plans for the single currency, however, he faced difficulty in securing the necessary support in Germany.

The events of 1989 were a seismic upheaval. With the disintegration of the Soviet bloc, which opened up the prospect of enlarging the Community to the East, German unification also became possible. But Kohl needed Mitterrand's support: both for formal reasons because France, as an occupying power, had the right to veto German unification; and, pursuing the policy initiated by Brandt, to ensure that new eastern relationships did not undermine the European Community and the Franco-German partnership. Mitterrand saw the single currency as the way to anchor Germany irrevocably in the Community system, and hence as a condition for German unification; and this ensured for Kohl the necessary support in Germany to proceed with the project.

The result was the Maastricht Treaty, which provided not only for the euro and the European Central Bank but also for other competences and institutional reforms. The Community was given some powers in the fields of education, youth, culture, and public health. Its institutions were strengthened in a number of ways, including more scope for qualified majority voting in the Council. The role of the European Parliament was enhanced through a 'co-decision' procedure that required its approval as well as that of the Council for laws in a number of fields; and it secured the right to approve – or not – the appointment of each new Commission. Two new 'pillars' were set up alongside the Community: one for a 'common foreign and security policy'; the other, relating to freedom of movement and internal security, for what was called 'cooperation in justice and home affairs' – renamed in the Amsterdam Treaty as 'police and judicial cooperation in criminal matters'. The basis for both was intergovernmental, though they were related to the Community institutions. The whole unwieldy

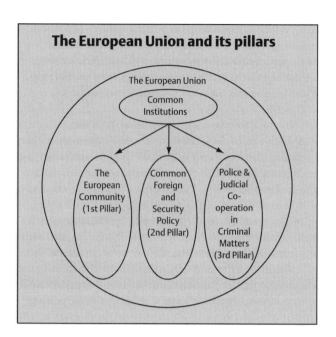

The European Union and its pillars

The European Union

Common Institutions

The European Community (1st Pillar)

Common Foreign and Security Policy (2nd Pillar)

Police & Judicial Co-operation in Criminal Matters (3rd Pillar)

structure was named the European Union, with the first, central, Community pillar as well as the other two.

Although John Major had succeeded Mrs Thatcher as Prime Minister with the avowed intention of moving to 'the heart of Europe', he insisted that Britain would participate neither in the single currency nor in a 'social chapter' on matters relating to employment. In order to secure agreement on the treaty as a whole, it was accepted that Britain could opt out of both, together with Denmark as far as the single currency was concerned.

The Maastricht Treaty was signed in February 1992 and entered into force in November 1993 after a number of vicissitudes: two Danish referendums, in the first of which it was rejected and in the second approved after some small adjustments had been made; a French referendum in which the voters accepted it by a tiny majority; in London, a fraught ratification process in the House of Commons; and in Germany, a lengthy deliberation by the Constitutional Court before it rejected a claim that the treaty was unconstitutional. These episodes, together with evidence that citizens' approval of the Union was declining in most member states, seemed alarming, particularly to people of federalist orientation.

The more federalist among the governments, however, felt that the Maastricht Treaty did not go far enough. With the decisive new monetary powers and the prospect of further enlargement, they wanted to make the Union more effective and democratic. By the time the Treaty entered into force, accession negotiations with Austria, Finland, and Sweden had already begun, and Cyprus, Malta, Norway, and Switzerland had lodged their applications. Norway negotiated an accession treaty but it was again rejected in a referendum; and the Swiss government withdrew its application after defeat in a referendum on the much looser European Economic Area. Negotiations with Cyprus and Malta were to begin in 1998 and 2001 at the same times as those with ten Central and East European states, following the European Council's decision that the latter could join when they fulfilled the economic and political conditions. But Austria, Finland, and Sweden acceded in 1995. So the Maastricht Treaty was followed in 1996 by another IGC, from which emerged the Amsterdam Treaty, signed in 1997 and in force in 1999.

The Amsterdam Treaty revisited a number of the Union's competences, including those relating to the two intergovernmental pillars. A new chapter on employment was added to the Community Treaty, reflecting concern about the unemployment that had persisted through the 1990s at a level around 10%, together with fears that it might be aggravated if the European Central Bank were to pursue a tight money policy.

Among the institutions, the European Parliament gained most, with co-decision extended to include the majority of legislative decisions, and the right of approval over the appointment not only of the Commission as a whole, but before that, of its President. Since the President, once approved, was given the right to accept or reject the nominations for the other members of the Commission, the Parliament's power over the Commission was considerably enhanced. Its part in the process that led to the Commission's resignation in March 1999 and in the appointment of the new Commission demonstrated the significance of parliamentary control over the executive. The treaty also gave the Commission's President more power over the other Commissioners.

At the same time as adding these federal elements to the institutions, the Amsterdam Treaty reflected fears that the Union would not be able to meet the challenges ahead if new developments were to be inhibited by the unanimity procedure. This led to a procedure of 'enhanced cooperation', allowing a group of member states to proceed with a project in which a minority did not wish to participate, though at the time of writing the procedure has not yet been used. Six weeks before the meeting of the European Council in Amsterdam that reached agreement on the treaty, Tony Blair became Prime Minister following Labour's election victory. The new British government adopted the social chapter and, expressing a more favourable attitude towards the Union, accepted without demur such reforms as the increase in the Parliament's powers. But Britain, along with Denmark and Ireland, did opt out of the provision to abolish frontier controls, along with the partial transfer of the related cooperation in justice and home affairs to the Community pillar, even if the British government was later to cooperate quite energetically in that field. As regards external security, Europe's weak performance in former Yugoslavia had spurred demands for a stronger defence capacity; and Britain both accepted provision for this in the Amsterdam Treaty and then joined with France to initiate action along these lines.

Enlargement to 27, Nice Treaty, Constitution

Following their emergence from Soviet domination, ten Central and East European states obtained association with the Union, and then sought accession. They faced an enormous task of transforming their economies and polities from centralized communist control to the market economies and pluralist democracies that membership required. But by 1997 the Union judged that five of them had made enough progress to justify starting accession negotiations in the following year; and negotiations with another five opened in January 2000. By 2004, accession was completed for the Czech Republic, Estonia, Hungary, Latvia, Lithuania, Poland, Slovakia, and Slovenia, together with Cyprus and Malta; and Bulgaria and Romania joined in 2007. Turkey's candidature was also recognized; but the economic and political problems were such that negotiations were not opened until 2005, were expected to take a decade or so, and were suspended in 2006.

With such a formidable enlargement ahead, the question of deepening arose again. Reform of some policies was necessary, in particular for agriculture and the structural funds. The Commission's proposals for this, entitled *Agenda 2000*, were partially adopted, though further measures were required. As regards reform of the institutions, another IGC was convened in 2000, leading to the Nice Treaty which was signed in 2001 and in force in 2002.

The result was an inadequate response to the prospect of nearly doubling the number of member states. It introduced modest increases in the scope of qualified majority voting in the Council and of legislative co-decision with the Parliament, and some procedural improvements for the Court of Justice. It addressed the growth in the number of Commissioners accompanying enlargement by further enhancing the power of the President over the other Commissioners and taking some steps to limit their number. But the weighting of votes in the Council and the number of MEPs for each state became the subject of unprincipled horse-trading, with an outcome that is not comprehensible to the vast majority of citizens. The German and Italian governments found the Treaty so unsatisfactory that they proposed a 'deeper and wider debate about the future of the Union'; and the European Council in December 2001, under Belgian Presidency, decided to establish a Convention to make further proposals to an IGC in 2004.

The Laeken Declaration, named after the Brussels suburb where the European Council met, was cleverly crafted to secure unanimous agreement by including, in what amounted to terms of reference for the Convention, items aimed at the more intergovernmentalist as well as the more federalist members. So the Convention met in February 2002 with a very broad remit, and its 105 members covered a wide spectrum of political orientations, with two MPs from each of the 27 member and candidate states plus Turkey as a forthcoming candidate, 16 MEPs, one representative of each head of government, two members of the European Commission, a President, and two Vice-Presidents.

The President of the Convention, former French President Valéry Giscard d'Estaing, steered a deft course between federalism and intergovernmentalism. The majority of its members, including MPs from member states, preferred a more federal than intergovernmental orientation; and Giscard satisfied them by favouring elements of federal reform within the Community pillar. But the amended EU Treaty drafted by the Convention would not be unanimously accepted by the ensuing IGC if the federal elements intruded too far into the fields of common foreign and security policy, and macroeconomic policy. Nor would some of the representatives of heads of government in the Convention have accepted the consensus that Giscard sought as the outcome of its work; and Giscard himself may well have sympathized with this view. So he steered the Convention towards more intergovernmental proposals in those fields. In July 2003 it acclaimed a consensus on a draft Constitution. Its main thrust was towards more effective and democratic institutions, as summarized at the end of Chapter 3. It also contained much tidying of the existing Treaty provisions for common policies and provided a basis for further development of a common defence. The IGC was convened in October 2003, agreed some amendments in an intergovernmental direction, and concluded a year later when all the member and acceding states signed the Treaty establishing a Constitution for Europe. Eighteen of them ratified the Treaty, but it was rejected by substantial majorities in French and Dutch referendums. While that signified the end of the Treaty as it stood, pressure remained for reviving as much of it as possible. The IGC approved the Treaty with a few amendments in October 2007, with the governments intending to secure ratification by 2009.

Chapter 3
How the EU is governed

The EU has major economic and environmental powers, and is increasingly active in foreign policy, defence, and internal security. How is this power used and controlled? How is the Union governed?

The answer, according to many intergovernmentalists, is through cooperation among the governments of member states: the other institutions are peripheral to the Council in which the governments are represented, and this fact will not go away. But while the Council is still the most powerful institution, federalists regard the Parliament, Commission, and Court of Justice not only as sufficiently independent of the states to have changed the nature of the relationships among them, but also as major actors in a process that may, and should, result in the Union becoming a federal polity.

The European Council and the Council

The Council consists of ministers representing the member states; and at the highest level there is the European Council of Heads of State or Government together with the President of the European Commission. Heads of state are included in the title because the Presidents of France and Finland participate as well as their prime

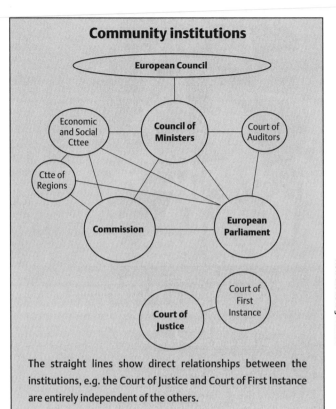

Community institutions

European Council

Economic and Social Cttee

Council of Ministers

Court of Auditors

Ctte of Regions

Commission

European Parliament

Court of First Instance

Court of Justice

The straight lines show direct relationships between the institutions, e.g. the Court of Justice and Court of First Instance are entirely independent of the others.

ministers, since they have some of the functions performed by heads of government elsewhere.

The European Council meets three or four times a year and takes decisions that require resolution or impulsion at that political level, sometimes because ministers have been unable to resolve an issue in the Council, sometimes because a package deal involving many subjects, such as a major amending treaty or a seven-year financial perspective, has to be assembled. The European Council

9. European Council 1979: facing different ways

also has to 'define general political guidelines'. Its rotating presidency is an important function, both for the management of current business and for launching new projects.

The meetings themselves are confined to three presidents (of France, Finland, and the Commission) and 27 heads of government, accompanied by foreign ministers, and sometimes finance ministers. But they are surrounded by a vast media circus which presents the results to the citizens of different countries in radically different ways. Thus readers of British newspapers could have been forgiven for supposing that the European Council in Helsinki in December 1999 was dominated by quarrels between Britain and France about beef and between Britain and the rest about proposals for a tax affecting the financial interests of the City of London. Yet beef was not on the agenda and tax took up only a little time. Many journalists in other countries emphasized the decisions to open entry negotiations with six more states and to establish a rapid reaction force to help with peacekeeping.

The 'Presidency Conclusions' are issued after each meeting, usually in a lengthy document, sometimes with bulky annexes. Of course the heads of state and government themselves initiate only a few of their decisions, and do not have time or inclination for thorough discussion of all that is put before them. They do initiate some major projects, as for example the rapid reaction force, which was a joint British and French proposal. But most of the detail and the 'political guidelines' emerge from the Union's institutions, working with the European Council's President-in-Office.

The Council of Ministers is a more complicated body. Which minister attends a given meeting depends on the subject. It meets in up to 15 forms, including an Economic and Financial Council (Ecofin), an Agriculture Council, a Justice and Home Affairs Council, and a General Affairs Council comprising the foreign ministers, which is supposed to coordinate the work of the other Councils, but is in practice hard put to it to control Councils of ministers from powerful departments of state. Each Council is, like the European Council, chaired by the representative of the state that is serving in turn for six months as President-in-Office.

Unlike the European Council, large numbers attend the meetings of the Council. Several officials as well as ministers or their representatives from each member state are present; and they are joined by the relevant Commissioners. Officials from the Commission also attend, as well as those from the Council Secretariat, which provides continuity from one presidency to the next and has become quite a powerful institution. Also unlike

10. Council of Ministers: not a cosy conclave

the European Council, much of the Council's work is legislative and some is executive.

After protracted pressure for the Council to hold its legislative sessions in public, it does have open sessions for all deliberations under co-decision and for its first deliberations under other legislative procedures. But its proceedings remain more like negotiations in a diplomatic conference than a debate in a normal democratic legislature.

The resemblance to an international negotiation was yet more pronounced before the mid-1980s when, with the launching of the single market programme, qualified majority voting (QMV) began to replace unanimity as the procedure for legislative decisions. Though the treaty stipulated that only texts proposed by the Commission could be enacted into law, the unanimity procedure had given each minister a veto with which to pressure the Commission into amending its proposal; and although the treaty provided for QMV on a range of subjects, the veto implicit in the Luxembourg 'compromise' extended its scope in practice to virtually the whole of legislation. The Committee of Permanent Representatives of the member states (called Coreper, after its French acronym) seeks common ground beforehand in the governments' reactions to the Commission's proposals; and given the difficulty of securing unanimity, it was thanks to the dedication of many of these officials that the Community was able to function at all. But measures identified by the Commission as being in the general interest and enjoying the support of a large majority were often reduced to a 'lowest common denominator', reached after long delay.

This contributed to the failure to make much progress towards the single market until the voting procedures were changed following the Single European Act. Up to then, single market measures had been passed at a rate of about one a month, barely enough to keep up with new developments in the economy, let alone complete the whole programme inside a quarter of a century. But the Single Act's provision for QMV on most of the single market legislation helped speed the rate to about one a week, putting the bulk of the laws in place by 1992.

The qualified majority among the 27 member states is 258 out of the total 345 weighted votes. The weights depend on size: France, Germany, Italy, and the UK have 29 votes each; Poland and Spain 27; Cyprus, Estonia, Latvia, Lithuania, and Slovenia have 4; Malta 3; and the rest are in between. Germany, with the biggest population, has the additional edge that the qualified majority will have to contain at least 62% of the Union's population, while to protect the smaller ones, at least a simple majority of states is required. This result of late-night bargaining in the Nice IGC was not designed for the EU citizens, who have to obey the laws and pay the taxes, to understand; and the Constitutional Convention had, as we shall see at the end of this chapter, a better idea.

While QMV is designed to ensure that laws wanted by a substantial majority can be passed, the Council still tries to avoid overriding a minority of one government about something it regards as important. This is due partly to the need to treat minorities with care in a diverse polity, as is the case in the Swiss federal system; and that motive has an edge in the EU, where a disgruntled government could retaliate by bringing business to a halt on other matters still subject to unanimity. Partly it reflects the diplomatic culture which prevails in the Council. But the difference between that and the 'Luxembourg veto' is that a vote is quite often taken, and proceedings take place in what has been called 'the shadow of the vote', so that ministers prefer to compromise than to run the risk that a vote will produce an outcome which is worse for them. Often the President, judging that a problem has been resolved, suggests that a consensus has been reached and, if there is no dissent, the Council accepts the text without a formal vote.

With the use of QMV for single market legislation, the Luxembourg veto began to fade away, so that QMV became the context for a wider range of decisions; and it was extended by the Maastricht, Amsterdam, and Nice Treaties to cover some four-fifths of all fields of legislation. The remaining one-fifth or so to which unanimity applied comes under a variety of headings. Britain was among those that insisted it apply to some aspects of employment-related social policy, for reasons of ideology as well as subsidiarity. Money, rather than ideology, was the motive of those who opposed QMV for decisions on the aims, tasks, and organization of the structural funds. There is British insistence on unanimity for tax harmonization, partly on grounds of sovereignty. Treaty amendments raising the ceiling for the Union's tax revenue and treaties of accession or even association have been held to touch sovereignty so closely that they must be ratified by each member state. While the Nice Treaty provided QMV for nomination of the President and other members of the Commission, and the Secretary General of the Council, the states have kept their veto over other major appointments such as Judges of the Court of Justice and Executive Board members of the European Central Bank, which have to be made by 'common accord' among the governments. Unanimity also prevails in the other two pillars, as Chapters 7 and 8 show.

The greater the number of member states, the harder it becomes to reach unanimous agreement. So in the context of enlargement, pressure grew to reduce the scope for the unanimity procedure, as the Nice Treaty indeed did to some extent; and this has been a source of conflict between those with more, or less, federalist orientation. A similar argument arises about the Council's executive role.

Unlike a legislative body in most democracies, the Council exercises significant executive powers. Although the Commission is, as Monnet envisaged, the Community's principal executive body, the Treaty allows the Council to 'impose requirements' on the way in which the Commission implements the laws, or even to see to their implementation itself. The Council disposes of a large number of committees of member states' officials to supervise the Commission's implementation and of 'working parties' to examine its legislative proposals, the whole network being controlled by Coreper. Each committee specializes in a branch of Community activity. They can be a useful means of liaison between the Commission and the states' administrations, to which the bulk of the execution of Community policies is in fact delegated. But the procedure that the Council has laid down for some of the committees makes it possible for officials from a minority of states to block the Commission's action until such time as the matter comes before the Council, which may then confirm the decision to block. This has led to complaints that the 'comitology', as the system is ironically called, undermines the Community's efficiency; and the Parliament, where it has the right to co-decide legislation, has used this to minimize the committees' blocking power. A committee may well be justified in resisting something the Commission wants to do in a particular case. But in general, it seems hardly credible that such a vast and complex matter as the execution of a wide range of the Community's policies could in effect be the responsibility of a body comprising the representatives of 27 separate governments.

The European Parliament

Members of the European Parliament (MEPs) are directly elected by citizens throughout the Union in June of every fifth year. There are 785 of them, distributed among the member states in proportions that favour the smaller states, though to a lesser degree than in the weighting of votes in the Council: ranging from 99 from Germany; 78 each from France, Italy, and the UK;

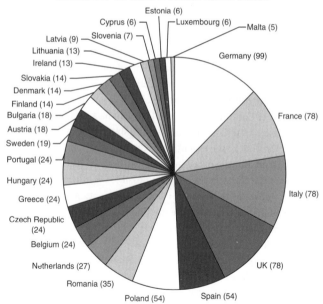

Number of MEPs from each state

Total number of MEPs: 785

and 54 each from Poland and Spain; down to 7 from Slovenia; 6 each from Cyprus, Estonia, and Luxembourg; and 5 from Malta.

The political culture of the European Parliament differs radically from that of the Council. The meetings are open to the public; voting by simple majority is the routine; and the MEPs usually vote by party group rather than by state. Three-quarters of the MEPs elected in June 2004 belonged to the mainstream party groups: 268 to the centre-right Christian Democrat and Conservative EPP (European People's Party) Group; 200 to the centre-left PES (Party of European Socialists) Group; and 88 to the ELDR (European Liberals, Democrats and Reformists) Group. The rest were evenly divided between smaller groups to the left, of which the most important were the Greens, and to the right, with a variety of eurosceptics – including a French party called 'Hunters and Fishermen', opposing EU legislation that affects those sports.

While agreement has not yet been reached on a uniform electoral procedure, or 'principles common to all member states' as the Amsterdam Treaty more tolerantly put it, all the states now operate systems of proportional representation. Until the 1999 European elections, Britain's first-past-the-post system caused violent swings in the balance between parties, reducing the number of Conservative MEPs from 60 in 1979 to 17 in 1994, while that of Labour rose from 17 to 62. But the proportional representation introduced by 1999 moderated the swing, returning 36 Conservatives and 29 Labour – together with 10 Liberal Democrats, compared with only 2 in 1994 from a larger share of the vote.

The balance between the mainstream parties has otherwise been fairly stable, with neither the centre-right nor the centre-left able to command a majority. So a broad coalition across the centre is needed to ensure a majority for voting on legislation or the budget; and this is all the more necessary for amending or

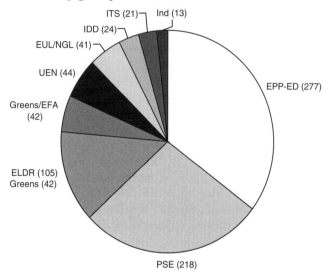

Party groups in the Parliament in 2007

ITS (21)
Ind (13)
IDD (24)
EUL/NGL (41)
UEN (44)
Greens/EFA (42)
ELDR (105)
Greens (42)
EPP-ED (277)
PSE (218)

Total number of MEPs: 785

EPP-ED	Group of the European People's Party and European Democrats
PES	Group of the Party of European Socialists
ELDR	Group of the European Liberal, Democratic and Reformist Party
Greens/EFA	Group of the Greens/European Free Alliance
UEN	Group of the Union for a Europe of Nations
EUL/NGL	Confederal Group of the European United Left/ Nordic Green Left
ID	Independence/Democracy Group
ITS	Identity, Tradition & Sovereignty Group
Ind	Independent

rejecting measures under the increasingly important co-decision procedure, where an absolute majority of 367 votes is required. The well-developed system of committees, each preparing the Parliament's positions and grilling the Commissioners in a field of the Union's activities, also tends to encourage consensual behaviour. But there has none the less been a sharper left–right division since the elections of 1999.

Although the Parliament has performed well enough in using its now considerable powers over legislation and the budget, the voters' turnout has declined with each election, from 63.0% in 1979 to 45.5% in 2004. One reason is a general trend of declining turnouts in elections within member states. Another is a widespread decline in support for the Union. Yet another may be that the Parliament in particular has been exposed to critical and, particularly in Britain, downright hostile media comment, fastening on matters such as the prolonged failure to establish an adequate system for controlling MEPs' expenses (largely the fault of MEPs themselves, though by now rectified), and the two costly buildings in Brussels and Strasbourg between which it commutes (entirely the fault of governments). Citizens may, moreover, not yet be aware of how much the Parliament's powers have grown, following the Maastricht, Amsterdam, and Nice Treaties.

The legislative role has developed from mere consultation at first, through the cooperation procedure initiated by the Single Act, to the co-decision introduced by the Maastricht Treaty and extended at Amsterdam and Nice to the point where it now applies to well over half the legislation. Already in 1989 the Parliament could use its influence under the cooperation procedure to secure results such as stricter standards for exhaust emissions from small cars. With co-decision its influence has greatly increased; and it has used its power of assent over association agreements as a sanction against human rights abuses in Turkey, and to ensure better conditions for Palestinians exporting to the Community from the occupied territories.

11. Elected representatives at work: European Parliament sitting

In a typical example of Union jargon that is hard for the public to understand, the budgetary expenditure is divided into CE (compulsory expenditure) and NCE (non-compulsory expenditure). The CE was opaquely defined as 'expenditure necessarily resulting from this Treaty or from acts adopted in accordance therewith' but was in fact designed to avoid parliamentary control over the agricultural expenditure, which France saw as a major national interest; and the Parliament has indeed fought to limit the growth of that part of the budget. But while its power over the CE is limited, the Parliament has the edge over the Council for the NCE, which, along with the expansion of the structural funds, has grown until it now accounts for over half the total expenditure. One example of the Parliament's use of its powers was the increase in the aid for economic transformation in Central and East European countries after they emerged from Soviet control.

While the Parliament's share of power to determine the budget is an essential element of democratic control, its role in supervising how the money is spent has had the greatest impact. As well as its power of scrutiny over the Commission's administrative and financial activities, the Parliament has the right to grant 'discharge': to approve – or not – the Commission's implementation of the previous year's budget, on the basis of a report from the Court of Auditors. If not satisfied, the Parliament withholds discharge until the Commission has undertaken to do what is required. Thus in 1992 it delayed the grant of discharge for the 1990 accounts until the Commission had agreed to allocate 50 members of its staff to an anti-fraud unit. In 1998, after the Parliament had withheld discharge for the 1996 accounts and was not satisfied with the Commission's response, it appointed a high-level expert committee to investigate in more detail. They produced a devastating report on mismanagement and some cases of corruption; and the Commission, anticipating the Parliament's use of its power of dismissal, resigned in March 1999.

The Parliament then used the powers it had gained in the Maastricht and Amsterdam Treaties over the appointment of the new Commission. First it made full use of its power over the appointment of the Commission's President, interviewing Romano Prodi to make sure he was a suitable choice for President, with acceptable policy orientations, then each of the nominated Commissioners, before approving the Commission as a whole. In 2004 it approved the nomination of José Manuel Barroso as President but refused to accept a Commission that included Rocco Buttiglione, because of the views he had expressed about women and homosexuals. Barroso then presented a list without him, and undertook, should Parliament withdraw its confidence from a Commissioner, either to require his resignation or formally justify a refusal to do so.

Having demonstrated its powers over both appointment and dismissal of the Commission, the Parliament is well placed to make clear to voters that it can in future use its influence to secure the appointment of a candidate for Commission President who reflects the results of European elections; and it has been suggested that a commitment by Parliament to do so could enhance voters' interest in the elections and thus strengthen the Union's representative democracy.

The Parliament shares power equally with the Council for over half of the enacted legislation and of the budget; and it has proved much better able than the Council to control the Commission. So it can be said that the Parliament is more than halfway towards fulfilling the functions of enacting legislation and controlling the executive, which a house of the citizens in a federal legislature would perform. The Council for its part would be akin to a house of the states, save that the unanimity procedure still applies to one-fifth of the legislation, many of its legislative sessions are not held in public, and it has retained executive powers that ill accord with its legislative role.

The Economic and Social Committee and the Committee of the Regions

Alongside the Parliament and the Council, the Community has two advisory bodies: the Economic and Social Committee (Ecosoc) and the Committee of the Regions. The Commission and Council must consult them on certain subjects specified by the treaty; the Commission, Council, or Parliament may consult them on any subject; and they can issue their 'opinions' on their own initiative. Both have 344 members, nominated by the states and appointed by the Council.

The members of Ecosoc represent a wide range of economic and social interests. Those of the Committee of the Regions are representatives of regional and local bodies. Both produce reports that are useful, though not usually influential. But with the influence that the German Länder already exert in Community affairs, and the growing strength of regional representation in other member states, of which the Scottish Parliament and Welsh

Assembly are notable examples, the Committee of the Regions may well gain more influence in future.

The European Commission

While the Commission, as it stands today, is not the federal executive that Monnet envisaged, it is, with its right of 'legislative initiative' and its functions in executing Community policies and as 'watchdog of the Treaty', a great deal more than the secretariat of an international organization.

The Treaty of Rome gives the Commission the sole right of legislative initiative, that is, to propose the texts for laws to the Parliament and the Council. The aim was to ensure that the laws would be based more on a view of the general interest of the Community and its citizens than would result from initiatives of the member state governments, and that there would be more coherence in the legislative programme than they or the Councils with their various functional responsibilities could provide. Armed with this power, the Commission was in its early days often called the 'motor of the Community'. After it had been weakened by de Gaulle's assault in the 1960s, the balance of power swung towards the Council and, since its establishment in 1974, the European Council. But the Commission still performs the essential role of initiating both particular measures for the Council and Parliament to decide, and general policy packages that the President-in-Office steers through the European Council. Outstanding examples of the latter were the 'Delors package' of budgetary reform that the European Council adopted in 1992 under British presidency, and the *Agenda 2000* reforms of Community policies to prepare for the Eastern enlargement that were agreed under German presidency in 1999; while the part played by the Commission in driving through the massive 'Bolkestein Directive' for completing the internal market for services demonstrated the essential part it continues to play in promoting the Union's development.

The Commission has also been called the 'watchdog' because it has to ensure that the Community's treaty and laws are applied, notably by the member states. If it has evidence of an infringement, it has to issue a 'reasoned opinion' to the state in question. Should the latter fail to comply, the Commission can take it to the Court of Justice. This is what happened in 1999 when the French government refused to accept the Community's decision that British beef was by then safe to eat and its import should be allowed. The Court found in the UK's favour in late 2001, although it was not until 2006 that the other member states agreed to lift restrictions, and fines were imposed on France by the Commission in excess of €10 million. The Commission is also responsible for executing Community law and policy, though much of it is delegated to member state governments and other agencies.

In order to ensure that the Commission works in the general interest of the Community, the treaty requires that its independence of any outside interests be 'beyond doubt'; and the Commissioners, on taking up office, have to make a 'solemn undertaking' to that effect. Although the treaty provides for their nomination by 'common accord' among the governments, each government has in the past made its own nomination and this has been accepted by the others. But this can no longer be taken for granted, because the accord of the Commission's newly appointed President is now also required before the Parliament's approval of the Commission as a whole.

Until 2005 there were two Commissioners from each of the larger and one from each of the smaller states. But the impending enlargement caused concern that a larger Commission would be less effective, so the Nice Treaty limited the number of Commissioners, as from 2005, to one from each member state. Proposals for a smaller number were stoutly resisted by smaller states such as Ireland. But the Treaty's Protocol on Enlargement provided that the number of Commissioners in the first Commission appointed after the accession of the 27th member state was to be fewer than the number of member states; and they were to be chosen with 'a rotation system based on equality'. So there will be tough negotiations between 2007, when Bulgaria and Romania joined, and the second half of 2009 before the next Commission starts work.

Reducing the number of Commissioners to fewer than one per state is by no means the only way to secure effectiveness. The top tier of governments, such as the British Cabinet, usually has over 20 members, in some cases over 30; and this has worked because a Prime Minister has the power to control the other members. The Amsterdam and Nice Treaties moved the Commission some way in that direction by giving the President the power not only to share in the decisions to nominate the other Commissioners, but also to exercise 'political guidance' over the Commissioners, to allocate and 'reshuffle' their responsibilities, to appoint

12. First meeting of the new Commission, 1999: President Prodi enjoys a laugh

Vice-Presidents, and to sack a Commissioner 'after obtaining the collective approval of the Commission'.

In treaty terminology, the Commission is the whole body of Commissioners. In common usage, it also refers to the Commission's staff. But it is usually clear whether reference is being made to the Commissioners or the 23,000 employees; and despite loose talk of a bloated bureaucracy, this is fewer than the numbers employed by many local authorities.

Since QMV now applies to the bulk of legislation, the Commission's sole right of initiative has given it a strong position in the legislative process. The Council can amend the Commission's text, but only by unanimity, which here works in the Commission's favour instead of against it, for while the Commission normally prefers to accommodate governments' wishes, it is better placed to resist their pressure on points it regards as important.

The Commission has performed its legislative role well. But its performance as an executive has been heavily criticized. Much of the criticism has been unfair, where the execution is in fact delegated to the member states. This is a good principle, which works well in Germany's federal system where the Länder administer most of the federal policies. But there the federal government has more power to ensure adequate performance from the Länder, whereas member states tend to resist the Commission's efforts to supervise them. The answer is surely not more direct administration by Brussels, but enough Commission staff to undertake the supervision and stronger powers to ensure proper implementation by the states.

The Commission has a good record in fields such as the administration of competition policy, where it was given the power to do the job itself and has done it well despite a shortage of officials. But there have been serious defects when it has been required to administer expenditure programmes without the staff who can do this properly, resulting in defects either in its own work or in that of consultants hired to do it, with sometimes bad and in a few cases fraudulent consequences.

Such defects, as well as those due to inadequate administrative practices and sense of financial responsibility, were among the criticisms of the report that led to the Commission's resignation in 1999 and to insistence that the new Commission must carry out radical administrative reform. The result included changes in recruitment, training, promotion, and disciplinary procedures; a new audit unit in the Commission to ensure funds are spent properly; and an 'inter-institutional committee' to oversee standards of behaviour in the Commission, the Council, and the Parliament.

Prodi was bold enough to suggest that the Commission is a European government. How far could this be this an accurate description? Within the fields of Community competence, its right of legislative initiative resembles that of a government, and even exceeds it in so far as the Commission's is a sole right. But its use of the right is constrained by the Council, particularly where the unanimity procedure applies, though also by the use of QMV rather than a simple majority. The difference is, however, greater in comparison with Britain than with states that practise a consensual style of coalition government. The Commission's executive role is constrained by the Council and the comitology but is otherwise not, in principle, far different from that of the German federal government, apart from the German government's more effective means of enforcing proper implementation by the Länder. A crucial distinction between the Commission and a government is, indeed, that the Commission does not control any physical means of enforcement. It has moreover only a minor role in general foreign policy, and very little in defence. Along with the differences, however, there are significant similarities.

13. Rule of law: the Court of Justice sitting

The Court of Justice

The rule of law has been key to the success of the European
Community. Increasingly, in its fields of competence, a framework
of law rather than relative power governs the relations between
member states and applies to their citizens. This establishes 'legal
certainty', which is prized by business people because it reduces
a major element of risk in their transactions. Politically, it has
helped to create the altogether new climate in which war between
the states is deemed to be unthinkable.

At the apex of the Community's legal system is the Court of
Justice, which the treaties require to ensure that 'the law',
comprising the treaties and legislation duly enacted by the
institutions, 'is observed'.

There is one judge from each member state, appointed for six-year
terms by common accord among the member states and whose

independence is to be 'beyond doubt'. The Court itself judges
cases such as those concerning the legality of Community acts,
or actions by the Commission against a member state or by one
member state against another, alleging failure to fulfil a treaty
obligation. But the vast majority of cases involving Community
law are those brought by individuals or companies against other
such legal persons or governments; and these are tried in the
member states' courts, coming before the Court of Justice only if
one of those courts asks it to interpret a point of law.

The Court's most fundamental judgments, delivered in the
1960s, were based on its determination to ensure that the law
was observed as the treaty required. The first, on the primacy
of Community law, was designed to ensure its even application
in all the member states; for the rule of law would progressively
disintegrate should it be overridden by divergent national laws.
The second, on direct effect, provided for individuals to claim
their rights under the treaty directly in the states' courts. Then in
1979 a judgment on the 'Cassis de Dijon' case laid a cornerstone
of the single market programme, with the principle of 'mutual
recognition' of member states' standards for the safety of products,
provided they were judged acceptable; and this radically reduced
the need for detailed regulation at the Community level. In 1985
the Court required the Council to fulfil its treaty obligation,
outstanding since 1968, to adopt a common transport policy; and
the Council duly complied.

The Court has by now delivered some 7,200 judgments, and
cases continue to come before it at a rate that makes it hard
to reduce the delays of up to two years before judgments are
reached. A 'Court of First Instance' was established to help
deal with this problem, hearing almost all cases brought by
individuals or legal persons, which relate mainly to competition
policy and to disputes between Community institutions and their
staff. But this has stemmed, not turned, the tide of cases awaiting
judgment.

While litigants can appeal from the Court of First Instance to the Court of Justice on points of law (hence the words 'first instance'), there is no appeal beyond the Court of Justice, which is the final judicial authority on matters within Community competence. To enforce its judgments, however, it depends on the enforcement agencies of the member states. The fact that the large majority of judgments under Community law are made by the states' own courts has instilled the habit of enforcing it; and there has been no refusal to enforce the judgments of the Court itself, even if there have sometimes been quite long delays before member states have complied with judgments that went against them.

The Court's jurisdiction is almost entirely confined to the fields of Community competence and, to some extent, the 'pillar' dealing with police and judicial cooperation. But within these limits, and apart from the almost total reliance on the member states' enforcement agencies, the Community's legal system has largely federal characteristics.

Subsidiarity and flexibility

In a speech delivered in Bruges in 1988, Mrs Thatcher famously evoked the spectre of a 'European super-state exercising a new dominance from Brussels'; and a 'slippery slope' leading towards a 'centralized super-state' has become a favourite metaphor for British eurosceptics. From a different starting point, German Länder have looked askance at proposals for Union competence in fields that belong to them in Germany's federal system. Indeed many federalists find the treaty objective of 'an ever closer union' too open-ended, and most support the principle of 'subsidiarity' as a guide to determine what the Union should do and what it should not do. That principle, which has both Calvinist and Catholic antecedents, requires bodies with responsibilities for larger areas to perform only the functions that those responsible for smaller areas within them cannot do for themselves. Following this principle, the treaty requires the Community to 'take action ... only if and insofar as the objective of the proposed action cannot be sufficiently achieved by the Member States', and can, 'by reason of its scale or effects, be better achieved by the Community'.

The Rome Treaty implicitly recognized this principle in distinguishing between two kinds of Community act: the Regulation, which is 'binding in its entirety' on all the member states; and the Directive, which is binding only 'as to the result to be achieved', leaving each state to choose the 'form and methods'. But this was a very partial application of the principle; and Directives were sometimes enacted in such detail as to leave little choice to the states. So the Maastricht Treaty defined subsidiarity and the Amsterdam Treaty laid down detailed procedures aiming to ensure that the principle would be practised by the Community institutions. Some federalists, finding this an insufficient safeguard against over-centralization, have proposed that the treaty should list competences reserved to member states. As a result of German pressure in particular, the constitutional Convention was required to propose a 'more precise delimitation' of powers between the Union and the states.

There are of course disagreements about the fields in which integration is justified. These left their mark on the Maastricht Treaty, in the British opt-outs from the social chapter and the single currency, and those of Denmark on the single currency and defence. Since the treaty can be amended only by unanimity, the other governments had to accept the opting-out if these items were to be included in it; and this led to growing interest in the idea of 'flexibility', enabling those states wanting further integration in a given field to proceed within the Community institutions or, to put it the other way round, letting a minority opt out. One purpose was to circumvent the veto of the UK or Denmark, where there was strong resistance to further integration. Although British policy changed somewhat after Labour's election victory in 1997, there is still British and Scandinavian resistance to some reforms which most other governments regard as necessary; and it is also feared that some of the new member states may prove unwilling or unable to proceed with further integration.

The concept of flexibility emerged in the Amsterdam Treaty under the heading of 'enhanced cooperation': a term preferred by federalists because it implied a deeper level of integration among a group of states, whereas eurosceptics tended to see flexibility as a way of loosening bonds in the Community as a whole. The Amsterdam Treaty provided for enhanced cooperation within the Community provided that a number of conditions were met, including unanimous agreement that it be applied in any given case, and the Nice Treaty allowed any group of eight or more states to proceed within the Union framework if a qualified majority consent.

Citizens

The concept of citizenship of the Union was introduced in the Maastricht Treaty, which provided that all nationals of the member states are also citizens of the Union; and the Amsterdam Treaty added that the two forms of citizenship are complementary. The Maastricht Treaty included a few new rights for the citizens, such as to move and reside freely throughout the Union subject to specified conditions, and to vote or stand in other member states in local and European, though not national, elections. This short list comes on top of specific rights already guaranteed by the treaties, such as protection for member states' citizens against discrimination based on nationality in fields of Community competence, and equal treatment for men and women in matters relating to employment. The Union's institutions are also required to respect fundamental rights, as guaranteed by the European Convention on Human Rights and Fundamental Freedoms. The Amsterdam Treaty affirmed that the Union is 'founded on the principles of liberty, democracy, respect for human rights and fundamental freedoms, and the rule of law, principles which are common to the member states'; and it went on to provide that, in the event of a 'serious and persistent breach' of these principles, a member state could be deprived of some of its rights under the treaty, including voting rights.

In response to concerns that the Union needs to do more to attract the support of its citizens, a Charter of Fundamental Rights was also drafted, in parallel with the IGC which prepared the Nice Treaty, by a Convention that set the precedent for the Convention which drafted the Constitutional Treaty. But the European Council, while 'welcoming' the Charter, did not include it in the Treaty, though the Court of Justice has referred to it in some of its judgments. The Treaty did, however, provide for the Parliament to appoint an Ombudsman to investigate citizens' complaints about maladministration by Community institutions and report the results to Parliament and the institution concerned.

Apart from the question of rights, the system for governing the Union, with its complex mix of intergovernmental and federal elements, makes decision-making difficult and a satisfactory relationship between the institutions and the citizens hard to achieve. Yet unless the citizens develop sufficient support for the Union alongside that for their own states, the states' electorates could become a centrifugal force leading to disintegration; and the enlargement to 27, probably eventually over 30, states presents additional problems. There has been lively academic discussion on the need for a Union demos to sustain a Union democracy, which has encouraged scepticism regarding its possibility. The Union has, however, been able to benefit from its growing democratic elements such as the powers of the European Parliament, and it is unduly pessimistic to assume that the process cannot continue, along with the development of the Union as a whole. The solidarity among citizens remains far short of what would be necessary for a federal state. Substantial further reform is, indeed, envisaged in the Reform Treaty approved by the IGC in October 2007.

Reform Treaty

Much of the comprehensive reform proposed in the Constitutional Treaty remains in the Reform Treaty approved by the European Council in October 2007 in a way that took account of the objections of member states; and even if not ratified by all of them, it may still indicate the direction of subsequent reforms, whether of the Union as a whole or of a substantial group of states such as the eurozone. The relationships between the institutions are to be simplified by abolishing the three-pillar structure introduced in the Maastricht Treaty; and this would be reflected in the Treaty structure, with a Treaty on the Functioning of the Union, based on parts of the Union's first pillar, alongside a Treaty on the European Union, the two together being designated the Reform Treaty.

The European Council is to fulfil its political responsibility for the strategic course of Union policy more coherently by electing a President for a two-and-a-half year period, renewable once, instead of rotating the post among the government heads of 27 or more member states. Nor would the President be distracted by holding any national office.

The Presidency of the Council is also to be reformed, though less radically, by the introduction of presidential trios of member states for 18-month periods, each holding the office for 6 months. The President of the Foreign Affairs Council would be appointed by the European Council, would be called the High Representative of the Union for Foreign Affairs and Security Policy, and would also serve as a Vice-President of the Commission in the interests of coherence for the Union's external policy as a whole. Qualified majority would be the Council's 'normal' legislative procedure, applying to over two-thirds instead of less than one-third of items. The allocation of a voting weight to each member state would be replaced by a general rule that a majority comprises 55% of the states containing 65% of the Union's population, though, in order to overcome Polish objections, that would not apply until 2014, with a minor exception until 2017.

The European Parliament is to be strengthened by extending co-decision to become, like QMV, the norm for Union legislation; and the distinction between 'compulsory' and 'non-compulsory' expenditure, which undermined the Parliament's control over agricultural spending, would be abolished. While the European Council is to continue to nominate the President of the Commission, it would be required to take account of the results of the European elections, and its nominee would be subject to election by the Parliament, which could help to give citizens a sharper sense of the political significance of voting in European elections. Along with the citizens' role in the Union's representative government, an element of direct democracy is to be introduced in the form of a requirement for the Commission to prepare a legislative proposal in response to a demand signed by a million citizens. The member states' parliaments could moreover object to a draft law on the grounds that it infringes the principle of subsidiarity, and if one-third of them did so, the Commission would have to reconsider its proposal.

The number of Commissioners is to be reduced to two-thirds that of the member states, by giving each state the right to nominate one for each of two Commissions out of three. Consonant with the abolition of the pillars, the role of the Commission in Justice and Home Affairs would be enhanced. Its power to ensure, together with the Court of Justice, that the member states comply with Union law would be strengthened. The Charter of Fundamental Rights is to be legally binding, save that it would not apply to UK domestic law; and the citizen's access to the Court would be improved. The Union's external role is to have a sounder juridical basis through giving it a single legal personality.

Along with the expanded role of the High Representative, the capacity for external action is to be augmented by a more explicit treaty base regarding climate change and energy solidarity, and by providing that a group of member states with the necessary military capability may establish permanent structured cooperation within the Union in the field of defence. Among the concessions to secure member states' acceptance to the mandate were those providing that the UK could opt into or out of policies concerning frontiers, asylum, and judicial cooperation, together with exemption from application of the Charter of Fundamental Rights to UK domestic law. The UK Independence Party should be pleased with the provision for negotiated secession from the Union.

Taken as a whole, the Reform Treaty comprises a broad agenda for making the Union more effective and democratic: a necessary counterpart for effective and democratic government in member states.

Chapter 4
Single market, single currency

While peace among the member states remained at the heart of the Community's purpose, from the second half of the 1950s a large common market became the focus for its action. The strength of the US economy was a striking example of the success of such a market; the Germans and the Dutch wanted liberal trade; and the French accepted the common market in industrial goods provided it was accompanied by the agricultural common market that would favour their own exports.

The idea of a large common market had a dynamic that endured through the subsequent decades, because it reflected the growing reality of economic interdependence. As technologies developed, and with them economies of scale, more and more firms of all sizes needed access to a large, secure market; and for the health of the economy and the benefit of the consumers, the market had to be big enough to provide scope for competition, even among the largest firms. So as the European economies developed, the EEC's original project, centred on abolition of tariffs in a customs union, was succeeded in the 1980s by the single market programme, then in the 1990s by the single currency.

There were both economic and political motives for each of the three projects: the benefits of economic rationality; and the consolidation of the Community system as a framework for peaceful relations among the member states. Economics and politics were also both involved in the substance and outcomes of the projects, because the integration of modern economies requires a framework of law, and hence common political and judicial institutions. Nor would success in either the economic or the political field alone have been enough to sustain the Community. There had to be success in both, which the customs union and the single market each achieved. It was also a combination of economic and political motives that secured the launch of the single currency, though not yet the participation of all member states.

The single market

Tariffs and import quotas were, in the 1950s, still the principal barriers to trade. The international process of reducing them began under American leadership in the Gatt (General Agreement on Tariffs and Trade). But the member states of the Community wanted to do more. The result was the EEC's customs union, abolishing tariff and quota barriers to their mutual trade, and creating a common external tariff.

Customs union, competition policy

Tariffs and quotas on trade between the member states were removed by stages between 1958 and 1968. Industry responded positively and trade across the frontiers grew rapidly, more than doubling during the decade.

While tariffs and quotas were the main distortions impeding trade, they were not the only ones. The Community was also given powers to forbid restrictive practices and abuse of dominant positions in the private sector. The treaty gave the task to the Commission, without intervention by member state governments; and in 1989 the Commission was also given the power to control mergers and acquisitions big enough to pose a threat to competition in the Community. Armed with these powers, the Commission has done much to discourage anti-competitive behaviour and has been seen as the toughest cartel-buster in the world. Thus in the first quarter of 2007, it fined Siemens €397 million and ThyssenKrupp €479.7 million for their activity in price-fixing cartels. Because of the volume of work, the Commission sought to return some of these responsibilities to the member states' competition authorities. There was pressure from business interests to prevent this, because they find it convenient to have the Commission as a 'one-stop shop', but some degree of decentralization did occur with the creation of the European Competition Network, in which the Commission and national authorities share information and coordinate investigations.

Unfair competition can also take the form of subsidies given by a member state government to a firm or sector (in the EU jargon 'state aids'), enabling it to undercut efficient competitors and undermine their viability. The Commission has been given the power to forbid such subsidies. But it has been harder to control governments than firms. The Commission has been able to enforce some difficult decisions on reluctant governments; but especially in the 1970s, after it had been weakened by de Gaulle and with the economies hard hit by recession, it could do little to stem the rising tide of subsidies.

Along with the subsidies, non-tariff barriers proliferated in those years, becoming the main obstacle to trade between member states. One reason was technological progress, generating complex regulations differing from one state to another. More important was pressure for protection from those who were suffering from the prevailing 'stagflation'. The European economy was indeed in bad shape, vividly evoked by the term 'eurosclerosis'. A way out was sought; and the Commission, together with leading business interests, persuaded governments that a programme to complete the Community's internal market was required.

Programme to complete the single market by 1992

With the success of the internal tariff disarmament in the 1960s in mind, some business leaders and members of the Commission's staff worked on the idea of a programme to remove the non-tariff barriers. When Delors became the Commission's President in 1985, he fastened onto this idea as the only major initiative that would be supported by the governments of all the member states: the majority because of its economic merits and the political aim of 'relaunching the Community' after two rather stagnant decades; Mrs Thatcher because of economic liberalization alone. But she did the Community the service of nominating the highly capable Lord Cockfield, who had been trade minister in her Cabinet, as a Commissioner to work with Delors on the project.

Delors and Cockfield put the project to the European Council in June 1985. Whereas the programme for eliminating tariffs in the 1960s could be specified in the treaty in the form of percentage reductions, the removal of non-tariff barriers required a vast programme of Community legislation. Frontier formalities and discrimination resulting from standards and regulations, from public purchasing, and from anomalies in indirect taxation all had to be tackled. The Commission published a White Paper specifying that some 300 measures would have to be enacted and proposing a timetable for completing the programme within eight years. This was approved by the European Council and incorporated in the Single European Act, making completion of the programme by the end of 1992 a treaty obligation.

The removal of non-tariff barriers was already implicit in the Rome Treaty, which prohibited 'all measures having equivalent effect' to import quotas. But because the practice of voting by unanimity had impeded the legislative process, the Single Act provided for qualified majority voting on most of the measures needed to complete the programme. The Commission also reduced the legislative burden by building on the principle of mutual recognition that the Court had established by its judgment in the Cassis de Dijon case, and by delegating decisions on much of the detail to existing standards institutes. Nevertheless, the single market remained a huge enterprise, surely one of the greatest programmes of legislation liberalizing trade in the history of the world.

It was an outstanding success. The latter half of the 1980s was a period of economic regeneration in the Community. While one cannot be sure how much of that was due to the single market programme, economic research has given it at least some of the credit. The programme certainly contributed to the recovery by generating positive views of business prospects as well as stimulating trade, together with structural reform exemplified by a spate of cross-border mergers. The industrially less-developed states – Greece, Portugal, and, at that time, Ireland and Spain – fearing they would be damaged by stronger competitors, had secured a doubling of the structural funds to help them adjust; and they too, assisted by this and by the expanding Community economy, benefited from the programme.

Politically, the single market enjoyed a remarkable degree of approval across the spectrum from federalists to eurosceptics. It has been a classic example of a purpose that is, as the treaty's article on subsidiarity puts it, 'by reason of scale ... better achieved by the Community'. The legislative framework has guaranteed producers a very large market and given the consumer a reasonable assurance of competitive behaviour among them. The Commission, Council, and Parliament were strengthened by their successful output, comprising a large part of the vast 'acquis', as the jargon puts it, of Community legislation; and the role of the Court was accordingly enhanced.

The programme was largely completed, but significant gaps still remain. The most notable area of difficulties has been in

Non-tariff barriers

When the Community was founded, the main barriers to trade were tariffs and quotas, and the Rome Treaty provided for their abolition in trade between member states. The Treaty also banned 'measures having equivalent effect', i.e. other barriers, generally known as non-tariff barriers (NTBs), which might not be expressly designed to limit trade but would actually have that effect. These include divergent standards or regulations on goods and services in the different states; frontier controls on goods and people; some discriminatory indirect taxes; and national preference by public purchasing authorities and state enterprises. The Treaty also provided for control of government subsidies to firms or individual sectors, to prevent unfair competition with more efficient enterprises in other member states.

As technologies developed and the economies became more complex, NTBs proliferated; and in the recessions of the 1970s governments resorted to them and to subsidies as protective devices. This led to the project to complete the single market through a vast programme of legislation to tackle NTBs. The bulk of the programme was completed as planned by the end of 1992, though the continual creation of new barriers meant that the Commission still is actively working to remove them.

the field of liberalization of services. Despite representing over two-thirds of EU GDP, there is little cross-border provision, not least because of fears in old member states about cheap labour coming from Central and Eastern Europe. This was seen most vividly in the French referendum campaign on the Constitutional Treaty in 2005, when the 'Bolkestein Directive', which aimed to liberalize services within the Union, became a symbol of social dumping, and the 'Polish plumber' an object of intense political concern. When the Bolkestein Directive was agreed in 2006, it had undergone much modification, weakening its impact.

The single currency

A monetary union requires that money in all its forms can move freely across the frontiers between member states and that changes of exchange rates between them are abolished. The single market programme went far to fulfil the first requirement and the Exchange Rate Mechanism prepared the ground for the second.

The ERM and monetary stability

The Exchange Rate Mechanism (ERM) was established in 1979, after the abortive attempt to move to monetary union in the 1970s. It required the central banks to intervene in the currency markets to keep fluctuations of their mutual exchange rates within narrow bands; and by the end of the 1980s it had, with the German Bundesbank as anchor, achieved a strong record of monetary stability. Here again, Britain stood aside at the start, only to join in 1990, at too high a rate and without the experience of the preceding decade of cooperation. In September 1992, currency turmoil forced the pound out of the ERM on what became known as Black Wednesday, making monetary integration a traumatic subject for many British politicians.

The ERM had the opposite effect in other member states. Most politicians as well as business organizations, having experienced the benefits of stable exchange rates, favoured the single currency. So did most trade unions. The costs of exchange-rate transactions, estimated at ecu 13–19 billion a year, which bear particularly hard on individuals and smaller firms, would be eliminated. But removal of the longer-term risks of exchange-rate instability would be the main economic benefit, definitively eliminating the exchange-rate risk, not just from trade but also, most significantly, from cross-border investments and from those that depend on reliable access to the Union-wide market: both of growing importance for the European economy.

Almost all the governments supported the single currency project, on grounds that reflected long-standing attitudes towards the Community. The most powerful commitment was in France, where a tradition of support for exchange-rate stability was bolstered by the desire to share in the control of a European central bank and thus recover some of the monetary autonomy that had in practice been lost to the Bundesbank. The French had also long wanted to equip Europe to challenge the global hegemony of the dollar; and in 1990 the single currency, already a keystone of the French political project for anchoring Germany in a united Europe, became for France an urgent necessity to respond to German unification. Other member states, apart from Denmark and the UK, accepted both political and economic arguments. For Germany, however, while the political motive for accepting the single currency as a French condition of unification was decisive, there were still reservations about replacing the deutschmark, with its well-earned strength and stability, by an unproven currency.

The success of the Bundesbank in securing monetary stability had demonstrated the merits of Germany's monetary arrangements. So other governments were ready to accept the German model for monetary union. For Germans, with their doubts about giving up the deutschmark, this was a *sine qua non*. They also continued to insist that monetary union alone was not enough, but that 'economic union' was required as well, with macroeconomic policies conducive to monetary stability.

The aim of economic and monetary union

The Maastricht Treaty, in providing for economic and monetary union (Emu), established the European Central Bank (ECB) to be, like the Bundesbank, completely independent. The ECB and the central banks of the member states are together called the European System of Central Banks (ESCB). The six members of the ECB's Executive Board, together with the governors of the other central banks, comprise the Governing Council of the ECB; and none of these banks, nor any member of their decision-making organs, is to take instructions from any other body. The 'primary objective' of the ESCB is 'to maintain price stability' though, subject to that overriding requirement, it is also to support the Community's 'general economic policies'. The ECB has the sole right to authorize the issue of notes, and to approve the quantity of coins issued by the states' mints. In response to German preference, the single currency was named the euro, rather than the French-sounding ecu.

In order to ensure that only states which had achieved monetary stability should participate in the euro, five 'convergence criteria' were established, regarding rates of inflation and of interest, ceilings for budget deficits and for total public debt, and stability of exchange rates. Budget deficits, for example, were not to exceed 3% of GDP and public debt was to be limited to 60% of GDP, unless it was 'sufficiently diminishing' and approaching the limit 'at a satisfactory pace'. Only states that had satisfied the criteria were to be allowed to participate; and once again, stages and a timetable were fixed, in order to give at least a minimum number of states the time to do so. Others were to have 'derogations' until they satisfied the criteria, while the British and Danes negotiated opt-outs allowing them to remain outside unless they should choose to join.

In the first stage all were to accept the ERM, as Britain had briefly done before being ejected by market forces. In the second stage they were to make enough progress to satisfy the convergence criteria. The third stage began in January 1999 with the 'irrevocable fixing of exchange rates' among the participating states, leading in 2002 to the introduction of the new euro notes and coins which replaced the participants' currencies entirely.

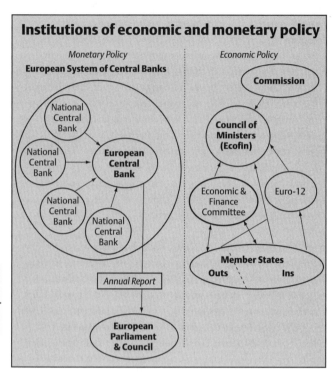

Institutions of economic and monetary policy

Monetary Policy
European System of Central Banks

- National Central Bank
- National Central Bank
- National Central Bank
- National Central Bank
- **European Central Bank**

Annual Report

European Parliament & Council

Economic Policy

Commission

Council of Ministers (Ecofin)

Economic & Finance Committee

Euro-12

Member States
Outs   Ins

During the mid-1990s, there had been much concern about which countries would be able to achieve the convergence criteria, partly for economic reasons (as with the case of Italy) and partly owing to more political factors relating to the degree of strictness with which the criteria would be interpreted by the EU. In the event, an economic upswing and strong political pressure allowed 11 of the 13 states to join in 1999, with only Greece being specifically excluded (although it was given the green light one year later), while the Swedish government had decided that membership was not politically viable and had asked not to move forward without its approval.

14. The euro: notes and coins

Thus by 2002 the very large majority of member states were eurozone participants and the issue of relations with those outside became a matter of some concern, because of the binary model of economic policy coordination it required. At least formally, all member states are committed to eventual membership, but in practice the lack of popular support in the UK, Denmark, and Sweden means that the situation is likely to persist for the medium term. In the UK, the government has effectively parked the issue for the foreseeable future, with its five conditions, as laid out by then-Chancellor Gordon Brown in 1999. These conditions relate to structural convergence, sufficient flexibility in eurozone economies, and the impact on various economic markers, but are suitably vague in their formulation, allowing any future government to make a decision on the basis of political factors. This was particularly important given the cross-party agreement that any decision would be made after a popular referendum.

The ambivalence of these three member states has been mirrored to a certain extent by newer members. While Slovenia was able to join the eurozone in 2007 (along with Malta and Cyprus from 2008), a number of other states have reined in some of their initial drive towards participation. Here the factors relate more to the economic flexibility that retaining a national currency allows, rather than any particular sense of the currency as a strong symbol of national identity. Moreover, all new member states are legally bound to introduce the euro as soon as possible, not having the opt-outs of the UK and Denmark.

Questions raised by Emu

Following the introduction of the euro, four major questions need to be addressed: the macroeconomic effect on the Union and the several states; accountability; the political consequences; and external monetary relations, which are considered in Chapter 10.

The argument about Emu's macroeconomic effects on the eurozone has followed the classic dichotomy between the prevention of inflation and of deflation. The value of the convergence criteria in this was recognized in their permanent embedding in a Stability and Growth Pact agreed in the Amsterdam Treaty, which sought to ensure that all member states would engage in economic policy-making that would support the cohesion of the Union as a whole.

The Stability and Growth Pact introduced an 'excessive deficit' procedure that allowed states to be fined for poor economic management. However, this came at a time of an economic downturn. France and Germany failed to curb their deficits sufficiently and demanded a revision of the Pact, much to the disgust of the Netherlands; and this led to the Pact's reform in

2005, essentially weakening its potential impact. Consequently, the Union has increasingly focused on other means of dealing with those 'asymmetric shocks' that have an uneven impact on member states.

The main attempt to ensure this has been the Lisbon Agenda. At the March 2000 Lisbon European Council, member states agreed an ambitious programme of structural reforms with the aim of creating 'the most dynamic and competitive knowledge-based economy in the world' by 2010, by means of policies tackling unemployment, increased use of technology, and more market liberalization and deregulation. That aim did stimulate some progress, particularly within smaller states. But while the 'open method of coordination', which dispenses with the common instruments and legally binding commitments of the Community method, is suitable for those fields within the programme where the subsidiarity principle indicates that sovereignty should remain with the member states, it has little capacity to resist the centrifugal forces of domestic politics, particularly in the larger states, or of unforeseen shocks; and with the end of the dot.com bubble, national politicians retreated into more protectionist positions, thus undermining the ability of the Union to make the most of the benefits of the single currency. In other fields, the Community method is much more reliable.

There is also concern about differing economic cycles within the eurozone. Interest rates at levels that suit the average will not be optimal for states with inflationary pressures above or below the average; and this is a downside to set against the general benefits of Emu. But the suggestion that the British cycle has to follow that of the United States, and so differs structurally from the average in the eurozone, does not fit well with the facts that nearly 60% of British exports of goods go to the EU, compared with 13% to the US, and that cross-Channel investment has been growing fast. Nor is the economic cycle a force of nature that cannot be influenced by government policy aiming at adequate convergence.

The independence of a central bank being a new experience for all except the Germans, the question of the ECB's accountability has also been raised. The treaty requires it to address an annual report to the Community institutions; its President has to present the report in person to the Council and the Parliament; and the President and other members of the ECB's Board attend meetings of the Parliament's relevant committees. The system is similar to that of the United States, save that the Joint Economic Policy Committee of the Congress has over the years become a powerful body disposing of a big budget to provide it with the necessary economic analysis and advice. The European Parliament's Finance Committee should surely move in that direction.

This leads to the question of the implications of Emu for the EU's powers and institutions. It is often suggested that far-reaching tax harmonization will have to follow. But the principle of subsidiarity requires that member states choose the pattern of their own taxes unless this has an 'external effect' on other member states. Thus minimum rates of added-value tax and excise taxes were fixed as part of the single market programme, in order to prevent unfair competition should a state adopt unduly low rates. Emu strengthens the case for similar treatment of taxes that affect competition in the capital markets. But beyond that there is no need to harmonize tax rates. There is a case for a fund for use on the infrequent occasions when there are serious asymmetric shocks; and there is a strong case for reforming the institutions so as to enable the Union to conduct an effective external monetary policy. But in general the EU has, with the single market legislation, the single currency, and its budget, the main instruments of economic policy to be found in federal systems. Its need is not more instruments, so much as to make the most of those it has: to ensure the full completion of the single market; to secure the participation of all member states in the eurozone; and to provide a budget large enough to finance what the Union can do more effectively than the several member states.

Another suggestion is that Emu will lead inevitably to a federal state. But a federal state has to have power over armed forces; and this does not follow from the adoption of the euro. The argument about defence integration, which is addressed later, is a different one. As regards strengthening the institutions and making them more democratic, that is already desirable, with or without the single currency; and it will become essential if the Union is to be capable of satisfying its citizens' needs and avoid the risk of disintegration. The euro adds to the case for radical institutional reform, but is not the central motivating force.

Chapter 5
Agriculture, regions, budget: conflicts over who gets what

The single market is a positive-sum game. Because it enhances productivity in the economy, there is benefit for most people, whether they take it in the form of consuming more or working less. But alongside the majority who gain, there will be some who lose, or at least fear they will lose, from the opening of markets to new competition; and these may demand compensation for agreeing to participate in the new arrangements. Such compensation usually has implications for the Community budget and looks like a zero-sum game, which can lead to conflict between those who pay and those who receive, even if the package of compensation and competition, taken together, benefits both parties. The first major example was the inclusion of agriculture in the EEC's common market.

Agriculture

The opening of the Community's market to trade in manufactures was, when the EEC was founded, a relatively simple matter of eliminating tariffs and quotas by stages. But tariff and quota disarmament was only a small part of the problem of creating an agricultural common market. All European countries managed their agricultural markets with complex devices such as subsidies and price supports to ensure adequate incomes for farmers and security of food supplies. So a common market for agriculture would have to be a complicated managed market for the Community, to replace those of the member states. It would have been simpler to confine the common market to industry. But the French feared the prospect of German industrial competition and, having a competitive agricultural sector, insisted that the Community market be opened to agriculture too.

High prices and Thatcher's 'money back'

The result was the common agricultural policy, with prices of the main products supported at levels decided by the Council of agriculture ministers, through variable levies on imports from outside the Community and purchase of surplus production into storage at the support level. Farmers' incomes were bolstered by high prices paid by the consumer, together with subsidies from the Community's taxpayers to finance the surpluses that the high prices evoked. While this was tenable in the Community's early years, once the UK became a member new tensions arose. The British model of free trade had meant that prices had been much lower, so membership of the common agricultural policy (CAP) meant a triple blow of higher prices for food, high levels of British contributions to the budget, because of import levies on foodstuffs, and low receipts from the budget, because of the small size of its agricultural sector.

This state of affairs was to trigger a five-year battle after Mrs Thatcher became Prime Minister in 1979, blocking much other Community business as her method of what she called 'getting our money back'. Matters came to a head in 1984, when the accumulation of stocks such as 'butter mountains' and 'wine lakes' had cost so much that the Community needed to raise the ceiling for its revenue from taxation; and this required unanimous agreement by the member states. So a deal was done, with agreement on a higher ceiling for tax resources allocated to the Community and an annual rebate for Britain at around two-thirds of its net contribution. At the same time a step was taken to reform the CAP, but only a modest step, because attention had been focused on the questions of the rebate and the tax resources.

Stages of reform

The CAP lumbered on, accumulating further costly surpluses, until 1988 when the money ran out again. This time the financial interests of member states prevailed. With the division of the Council into functional formations, the decisions of the Council of agriculture ministers on prices of farm products had determined the level of the bulk of Community expenditure, over which the Council of finance ministers had little say. Since the resulting bill had to be paid out of the Community's tax resources, the agriculture ministers were in effect deciding on the rate of tax paid by the citizens to the Community. Financial control had to be established and the European Council agreed in 1988 on a package of measures, proposed by Delors, which introduced a 'financial perspective' setting limits for the main headings of the Community's expenditure during the five years 1988–92. The growth of spending on agriculture was restricted to less than three-quarters of the rate of growth of the total.

While this took some of the heat out of the conflict over money, a serious reform of the CAP was still required. By 1992 the Commissioner responsible for agriculture was Ray MacSharry, a former Irish minister. He grasped the nettle and, outmanœuvring the opposing interests, secured a cut of 15% in the support price for beef and nearly one-third for cereals. The current levels of expenditure were not reduced, because farmers were compensated with income supports, including 'set-aside' payments for leaving cultivated land to lie fallow. But the measures removed the expansionary dynamic from the CAP and prepared the ground for further reform.

The cost of the CAP remained a heavy burden for the Community, with half the budget going to support a sector that employs

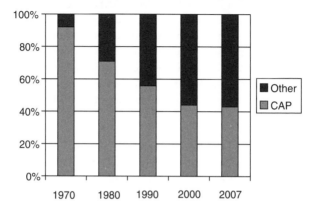

Share of budget spent on CAP, 1970–2007
(*percentage of total budget*)

less than 5% of the working population, much of it for a small minority of the bigger and richer farmers. By the end of the 1990s, moreover, the twin pressures of enlargement to the East and negotiations in the newly established World Trade Organization (WTO) were forcing the EU into a more structural reform process. New member states, with their large agricultural sectors, were set to drive up costs very significantly, while the need to secure agreement in WTO trade liberalization negotiations was placing increasing pressure on reductions in levels of agricultural support. Consequently, the Union agreed substantial cuts for some products in 1999, as part of wider budgetary negotiations, as well as introducing the notion of a multifunctional CAP, i.e. one that extends into the social and environmental dimensions that surround farming. This recasting of CAP as a 'rural' policy was an important step in helping to unblock the reforms that some states, notably France, had put on hold.

This became much more apparent at the 'Mid-Term Review' of the 1999 agreement in 2003, with what had initially been considered a simple review of the changes producing reforms as important as those of MacSharry a decade previously. Again the amount of price support was cut, but the main revolution was the shift to direct support for farmers. Until then, CAP had used price support mechanisms to pay farmers, thus providing a strong incentive to over-produce: hence the wine lakes and butter mountains of the 1980s. The new Single Farm Payment (SFP) introduced in 2006 separates (or 'decouples' in the jargon) payment from production: instead farmers are paid to look after their land, regardless of whether they choose to farm it or not.

The breaking of the old model of price support was perhaps inevitable in the face of the pressures that CAP had faced over the previous 40 years. The combination of enlargement, WTO negotiations, rising environmental concerns, and public health scares ultimately proved too powerful to resist. What is still not clear is how CAP will develop in the medium term: the new member states are natural supporters of a substantial CAP that pays their farmers well, while the notion of a more multifunctional approach to rural development has become a much more dominant discourse within the institutions. Either way, it would appear that CAP is set to experience yet more change.

Cohesion and structural funds

The 'cohesion policy', the other big item of expenditure in the Community's budget, has been a happier experience than the CAP. It stems from fears in member states with weaker economies that they would lose in free competition within the Community. When the customs union, the single market, and the single currency were established, funds were provided to assist their economic development so that they would cooperate in these new ventures and become prosperous partners: hence the word 'cohesion'.

Italy and Britain: Social Fund and Regional Development Fund

The first such provision was for the Social Fund, included at Italy's request in the Treaty of Rome. Italy's economy was the weakest among the six founding states and Italians feared they would suffer from the liberalization of trade. They wanted a fund to help their workforce to adapt; and their demand was met, though on quite a small scale.

The motive for establishing the European Regional Development Fund (ERDF) was somewhat different. By the time of British accession in 1973, Britain's economic performance had fallen behind those of the six founder states; and there was the prospect of the big net contribution for the CAP. Britain had its share and more of regions with economic difficulties, but other member states had theirs too. Edward Heath's government, which had negotiated British accession, had the sound idea that a fund for regional assistance would both respond to a general interest and be of particular value to Britain, not only assisting its regional development but also reducing its net contribution to the Community budget. While the initial impact of the fund was weak, it has developed into the main source of financing for cohesion.

The third of what became known as the 'structural funds', in order to underline that their aim was not just to redistribute money but rather to improve economic performance in the weaker parts of the Community's economy, was the 'Guidance Section' of the European Agricultural Guarantee and Guidance Fund (EAGGF). The Guarantee Section, which finances the subsidies for price support, still outweighs the Guidance Section, whose purpose was to help farmers carry out structural change. But the three structural funds, though at first small, grew steadily and were available to respond to the demand for a major expansion in the 1980s when the Community was enlarged to the south.

Enlargement and structural funds

When Spain, Portugal, and Greece joined the Community, their average incomes were far below those of the other member states save Ireland, which before its phenomenal growth in the 1990s was at a similar level. These four countries, led by Spain, demanded a major increase in the structural funds. They evoked a ready response from Delors, who in the run-up to Spanish and Portuguese entry was steering the single market project through the Intergovernmental Conference that produced the Single European Act. He was strongly motivated by the idea of social justice; and, though the governments had various views on that subject, it was evident that four discontented states could cause difficulties for the passage of the single market legislation. So the Single Act contained an article on 'economic and social cohesion'; Delors proposed that the budget for the structural funds be doubled in the financial perspective for 1988–92; and this was accepted by the European Council.

A similar problem emerged when it was decided to embark on Emu, with the same four states seeking a similar expansion of the structural funds. This time Delors secured an increase of two-fifths in the allocation for the period 1993–9; and the Maastricht Treaty provided for the establishment of the Cohesion Fund, to support projects in the fields of the environment and transport infrastructure. By 2000 the budget for the funds was €32 billion.

The four states for which the expansion of the structural funds was originally designed have performed for the most part well. Spain has been very successful, though less outstandingly so than Ireland; and Greece has recovered after faltering for a number of years, whereas Portugal had to check its initially rapid growth with a stabilization programme. While it is not possible to say how much of this generally good result can be attributed to the

Structural funds and objectives

Since the early 1970s, the Community has developed its regional policies around a set of funds and objectives. These were reformed in 1999 and again in 2006.

The structural funds now comprise:

- the European Regional Development Fund (ERDF) – deals with regional development and economic change;
- the European Social Fund (ESF) – concerned with re-training workers;
- Cohesion Fund – aimed at poorer member states, this fund develops projects in the environment and infrastructure.

Since 2007, spending has been focused on three key objectives:

- Convergence (areas with GDP per head less than 75% of the EU average) – roughly €45 billion per year is spent helping regions with a population of 154 million;
- Regional Competitiveness & Employment (helping areas to make structural adjustments to meet new economic situations and to adjust labour forces) – €9 billion per year goes to regions with a population 314 million;
- European Territorial Cooperation (developing cross-border links between member states) – over €1 billion per year to help regions with 182 million people living in them.

structural funds, the contributions of 2–4% of GDP certainly eased the path.

Although the objectives of the structural funds had been focused on help for regions where development was 'lagging behind', it has always been a feature of cohesion policy that all member states get something back out of the budget. Partly this is a reflection of the diversity of the states, but it is also driven by the unanimity required to conclude budgetary planning negotiations. This posed a particular problem with the enlargement to the East, since under the policy that prevailed in the late 1990s, new member states stood to receive very large amounts of funding, while existing member states stood to lose out.

The response to this was, as with CAP, to engage in some fairly drastic reforms. The growth in funding for cohesion was capped in the financial perspective agreed at Berlin in 1999, since richer member states were not prepared to foot the bill, while simultaneously it was decided that most of the existing funding should be ring-fenced for existing members, regardless of new members' objective needs. Coupled with the Commission's pronouncement that transfers to any member state would be capped to the equivalent of 4% of GDP, on the grounds that this was the most any country would usefully absorb, when enlargement did come in 2004 its impacts on the budget were relatively attenuated. Despite average incomes in new member states being typically half to two-thirds the EU average, they receive only one-third of cohesion funding. While this proportion is more than the one-fifth of the EU's population that they represent, it is still less than would seem to be necessary to help them move reasonably fast towards comparable standards of economic development.

Thus while the cohesion policy has, unlike the CAP, been relatively harmonious, it is important to recognize the limitations that member states have placed on maximizing its benefit for the community as a whole. This posture has also increasingly affected the budget as a whole.

The budget

With agriculture now accounting for under half of EU expenditure and cohesion somewhat over one-third, the two together, with their powerfully redistributive effects, account for four-fifths. The cost of administration in the Union's institutions comes to less than 7% of the total, and the remainder goes to finance a range of internal and external policies. A major item of redistribution outside the budget is the rebate to reduce the British net contribution, which amounted in 2005 to €5.5 billion and is paid direct to Britain by the other member states.

The total expenditure in the budget for 2007 was €126.5 billion, or 1% of Union GNP. This has to remain below 1.24% of GNP unless that ceiling is increased by a decision ratified by all the member states; and the financial perspective for the years 2007–13 keeps spending below 1% of GNP in each year.

'Own resources'

Unlike international organizations that depend on contributions from their member states, the EU's revenue from taxes is a legal requirement under the treaty, subject, like other treaty obligations, to the authority of the Court of Justice. This is to prevent member states from holding the Union to ransom by withholding contributions. The consequences of such behaviour are demonstrated by the financial state of the United Nations, weakened for many years by the refusal of Congress to sanction payment of the due US contribution – ironically enough, since the failure of American states to pay their due contributions in the 1780s under the Articles of Confederation was a powerful argument in favour of the US federal constitution. The same argument influenced the EC's founding fathers to make the payment of tax revenue to the Community a legal obligation.

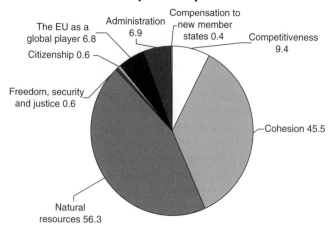

Breakdown of budget expenditure, 2007 (€ billion)

Administration 6.9

The EU as a global player 6.8

Citizenship 0.6

Freedom, security and justice 0.6

Compensation to new member states 0.4

Competitiveness 9.4

Cohesion 45.5

Natural resources 56.3

Total: €126.5 billion

The EU has no physical means of enforcement should a member state not hand over the money. But the rule of law has been of sufficient value to the member states to be respected by them.

Initially the EEC's tax revenue, called in the treaty 'own resources' to underline the point that they belong to the Community not the states, comprised the takings from customs duties and agricultural import levies. But these were not enough to pay for the CAP, and the Community was allocated a share of value-added tax at a rate of 1% of the value of the goods and services on which VAT is levied.

A major objection to these indirect taxes was that they bear hard on the poorer states and citizens, making them pay a higher proportion of incomes than the richer. So in 1988 a fourth

Sources of revenue, 2007

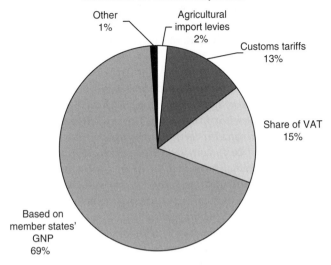

resource was introduced, in the form of a small percentage of the gross national product of each member state. This is roughly proportional to incomes and by 2007 accounted for over two-thirds of the EU's revenue. But the total outcome of the revenue system is still regressive.

Net contributions

As mentioned above, it was Mrs Thatcher who first coined the phrase 'our money back', although the British had, since their accession in 1973, been constantly seeking redress for what they could claim to be an 'unacceptable situation' resulting from a financial regulation adopted just before they joined. Previously, the fact that some member states got more out of the budget than others was taken simply as part of the package of membership. In particular, the Germans, who had willingly accepted for many years their role as the largest net contributor, did so because they recognized that the benefits of membership could not be measured simply by a bank balance: the country gained not only in deeply desired international acceptance and security, but also, more prosaically, in giving German exporters access to large new markets.

None the less, since the 1980s, and particularly since the mid-1990s, member states have become much more aware of the financial costs of membership. This was driven in part by Mrs Thatcher and her energetic campaign, but also by the development of Community and Union policies. The large growth of cohesion spending further reinforced the north-south divide between net contributors and recipients, while the growth in importance of the fourth resource effectively renationalized budgetary receipts. In addition, existing member states were concerned about the budgetary implications of enlargement. Coupled to Germany's increasing reluctance to foot the bills, reform became increasingly inevitable.

In 1999, the Berlin European Council agreed to reduce the amount that Germany, the Netherlands, Austria, and Sweden, the then net contributors, paid towards the British rebate. That rebate remained a bone of contention, since the original case of over-contributions and under-receipts was less and less compelling, but successive British governments were loath to give up an income stream of several billion pounds a year. None the less, as enlargement became a reality, the British did demonstrate some willingness to reduce the level of their rebate, in order to minimize the burden on the new member states, agreeing in 2005 to take a reduction of the rebate of €10.5 billion between 2007 and 2013, equivalent to roughly one-quarter of the total value. This was intended to help the British case for a more general review of spending policies and budgetary procedure, although there was very little to show for it other than a review of the budget in 2008–9.

States' net budgetary payments or receipts (*percentage of GDP, 2005, minus sign net payments*)

Netherlands	-0.52	Spain	0.68
Luxembourg	-0.36	Cyprus	0.69
Sweden	-0.30	Hungary	0.72
Germany	-0.27	Slovakia	0.73
Belgium	-0.20	Poland	0.80
France	-0.17	Ireland	0.83
Italy	-0.16	Estonia	1.54
Denmark	-0.13	Portugal	1.64
Austria	-0.11	Malta	2.07
United Kingdom	-0.08	Latvia	2.09
Finland	-0.05	Greece	2.19
Czech Republic	0.19	Lithuania	2.55
Slovenia	0.37		

Source: European Commission, *Allocation of 2005 EU Expenditure by Member States*, September 2005

Agriculture, regions, budget

Of more concern is the lack of growth in the EU's budget overall. Since 1999, there has been a reduction in the ceiling of expenditure as a percentage of GNP. Even with the growth of that GNP over time, the budget remains very small in comparison with member state governments' budgets. This is a somewhat unfair comparison, since the EU does not have to spend on social security, defence, health, education, or any of the major items that we typically associate with public activities. However, the size of the budget does constrain what the Union can do, for example in promoting cohesion and balanced development across all its member states. While it does appear to have weathered the transition to an enlarged membership, it is evident that further reforms will be needed if the Union is to remain a relevant actor, both internally and in the wider world.

Chapter 6

Social policy, environmental policy

The EU has been given some of its powers, such as those to establish the single market, because its size offers advantages that are beyond the reach of the individual member states. Other powers are designed to prevent member states from damaging each other. The environment is one field in which powers have been given to that end, with general agreement that it is desirable. Another is social policy, where there has been sharp disagreement as to how far EU intervention is required.

Social policy

The term 'social policy' has a narrower meaning in EU parlance than it generally has in Britain. It does not refer to the range of policies, including health, housing, and social services, with which the welfare state is concerned. The pattern of such services differs from country to country, reflecting their political and social cultures; and it is widely accepted that the cross-border effects of the differences are not sufficient to justify intervention by the Union. In the Treaty and EU jargon, however, social policy concerns matters relating to employment, where there are also wide variations from country to country. But since conditions of employment touch more closely on the single market, there has been pressure to harmonize member states' policies in order to prevent employees in states with higher standards suffering as a result of competition from those with lower standards.

The first such example was the article on equal pay in the Treaty of Rome. France was ahead of other founder states in having legislated that women be paid equally with men for equal work. In order to keep sectors that employed a high proportion of women competitive, France demanded that its partners introduce equal pay too. With the general movement towards gender equality, this was to become one of the most popular European laws. By the time of the Amsterdam Treaty, there was ready agreement to extend the principle from equal pay to equal opportunities and equal treatment in all matters relating to employment.

The Single European Act extended the scope of social policy in two directions: providing for legislation on health and safety at work and for the encouragement of dialogue between representatives of management and labour at European level. While Mrs Thatcher had fought hard against the influence of 'corporatist' relationships in Britain, she doubtless reckoned that such dialogue at European level would not be of much consequence; and the case against undercutting standards of health and safety was generally agreed. So although Community social policy was to become one of Thatcher's bêtes noires, she accepted these provisions of the Single Act as part of the package that included the single market programme.

In 1989 Delors, who saw higher standards of social legislation as being, for workers, a necessary counterpart to the single market, proposed a Social Charter that was approved by all but one in the European Council. Thatcher dissented. Although she accepted some of its provisions, such as free movement for workers and the right to join (or not) a trade union, she contested others, such as a right for workers to participate in companies' decision-taking, as well as maximum working hours – which, much to the British government's disgust, were subsequently enacted by a qualified

Social policy

Social policy in the EU jargon means policy relating to labour relations. It was the subject of a Protocol to the Maastricht Treaty, signed by all the member states save the UK, because the then British government did not accept it. The Labour government elected in May 1997, however, accepted it as a section of the Amsterdam Treaty.

EU social policy focuses on several areas: improvement of the working environment to protect workers' health and safety; working conditions; information and consultation of workers; equality between men and women at work; integration of people excluded from the labour market. This is done by supporting and co-ordinating national policies and by legislation, enacted in certain areas by co-decision between Council and Parliament. The Commission is required to encourage cooperation among member states in matters such as training, social security, accident prevention.

Amsterdam also authorized the Council, acting unanimously, to take action to combat discrimination 'based on sex, racial or ethnic origin, religion or belief, age or sexual orientation'.

majority vote under the treaty article on health and safety at work. Major followed her example when he secured Britain's opt-out from the provisions on social policy in the Maastricht Treaty, which therefore appeared in a protocol that applied to all the other member states. It was only after Labour's election victory in 1997 that there was unanimous agreement to convert the protocol into a social chapter in the Amsterdam Treaty; and it was accompanied by a new chapter aimed at achieving 'a high level of employment and of social protection'. But Britain has continued to promote the cause of flexible labour markets, an objective that was taken up in the Lisbon Agenda, which brought together social policy with employment policy in a combination that was much more oriented to the use of economic growth to provide for social well-being.

Flexibility or regulation in labour markets

Britain has emphasized deregulation and flexibility in its approach to the EU, on the grounds that it will make the European economy more competitive and increase employment. While labour markets are not the only sector of the economy in which deregulation is advocated, they are seen as among the most important.

While this British approach has been called 'Anglo-Saxon' because of similarities with American economic philosophy, an alternative became known as the 'Rhineland' approach, with Germany the leading example. There the emphasis in labour markets has been on solidarity and social protection rather than flexibility. Much of the regulation to achieve this has been negotiated between employers and unions, called in Germany the 'social partners'. This has reflected a culture of consensus in civil society in reaction against the ways of the preceding totalitarian dictatorship; and it has built on long-standing traditions of solidarity, such as the acceptance of responsibility in the private sector for the high standards of technical training. The results have included the outstanding economic success of the post-war decades and the continuing strength of German exports. But although the burden of integrating the eastern Länder into the German economy is one cause of the less successful performance in the 1990s, Germany is also criticized for reluctance to introduce more flexibility into the labour market and to reform industrial and financial organization and the tax system, in response to current developments in the global economy.

The Rhine also flows through the Netherlands; and the Dutch too have a highly consensual economic and political system.

Employment policy

The Amsterdam Treaty introduced a new section on employment in response to concern about the high level of unemployment in the EU. Its main purpose is to encourage cooperation among the member states with respect to their employment policies.

The member states provide annual reports on their employment policies to the Council and Commission, which draw up a report for the European Council. Guidelines are then issued to the states to be taken into account in their employment policies; and the Council can make recommendations to governments. The Council, in co-decision with the Parliament, may decide to spend money from the budget to encourage exchanges of information and best practices, provide comparative analysis and advice, promote innovative approaches, and fund pilot projects.

This has raised the profile of employment policy in the Union but it remains to be seen how much effect it has on governments' policies.

Faced with critical economic problems in the 1980s, they began a process of reform which led to what is called the 'Polder model', introducing market-oriented reforms into what remains a consensual system; and they achieved lower unemployment, higher efficiency, and a good all-round economic performance. Scandinavians have much in common with this approach.

The French, while stressing social protection, rely more on government leadership and regulation; and they too, despite criticism that they were slow to reform, performed well through the 1990s on most measures save their high rate of unemployment, which remained above 10% until 2007. But unemployment has remained particularly high among young people; and the economy became gradually less successful. So President Nicolas Sarkozy began to lighten the regulatory burden.

It is often forgotten that the British, for more than three decades after World War Two, had an economy that was highly regulated by both collective bargaining and government intervention. It was in reaction against this that the reforms of the Thatcher period moved Britain sharply towards the Anglo-Saxon model. While the intention of Blair's 'third way' was to prevent such oscillation by occupying a centre ground in between, much of the emphasis on economic flexibility and his government's enterprise-friendly orientation derived from his predecessors' reforms, as well as from an older British tradition of economic liberalism.

The improved British economic performance since the 1990s has helped to give credibility to the Anglo-Saxon approach, as has the dynamism of the Irish economy. But most important was the sustained success of the American economy, with its low unemployment and high growth, from which the conclusion could be drawn that flexibility suits the current stage of technological development. While the degree of laissez-faire in the American approach to social policy is resisted, a certain consensus may be emerging in the EU that methods such as bench-marking and peer pressure are more suitable than social legislation for reducing unemployment, as well as for some measures to create a dynamic and competitive economy. While there is still a strong constituency within several large member states for an interventionist approach to such questions, the rise of globalization and the need to maintain competitiveness have moved the debate within the Union towards the British viewpoint.

Environmental policy

Polluted air and water cannot be prevented from moving out of one state and causing damage in another. So there is an interest in common standards to control the pollution at its source. The same applies to the environmental effects of goods traded in the single market. The Single European Act provided for a Community environmental policy to deal with these problems. It also affirmed that the EC's objective was to 'preserve, protect and improve the quality of the environment'.

Over 300 environmental measures have been enacted, responding to a wide range of environmental concerns: air and water pollution; waste disposal; noise limits for aircraft and motor vehicles; wildlife habitats; quality standards for drinking and bathing water. In 1988 a law was passed to reduce the incidence of acid rain, cutting emissions of sulphur dioxide and nitrogen oxides by 58% by stages over the following 15 years. Standards of protection against dangerous chemicals were demanded following the accession of the environmentally conscious Swedes in 1995; and the highly complex REACH directive for guaranteeing standards throughout the Union was finally passed in 2006. While Community legislation had always allowed member states to set their own higher standards in other matters, Scandinavian pressure led to an article in the Amsterdam Treaty allowing states to have higher standards for traded products too, provided they can persuade the Commission that these are not protectionist devices; and by 2004, the 'polluter pays' principle became Community law. The focus on environmental policy came at a time when Europeans were rapidly becoming greener, so it became one of the Community's most popular policies, as the provision for equal pay had done before; and like policy for gender equality, it too was strengthened by the Amsterdam Treaty, which stipulated that 'environmental protection requirements' must be integrated into other Community policies 'with a view to promoting sustainable development'.

The Sixth Environmental Action Programme, which the Council and Parliament approved in 2002, contained a ten-year framework for promoting sustainable development, in the fields of climate change, nature and biodiversity, environment and health, and natural resources and waste. Later in that year the Union played a leading role in the World Summit on Sustainable Development in South Africa. Sustainable development strategy has subsequently been a priority, with climate change the most prominent element.

The Union's action with respect to climate change has had a powerful impact, both internally and in the wider world. The EU signed the Kyoto Protocol in 1998, with its target of cutting emissions of greenhouse gases by 2012 to 8% below the 1990 level. The Council then, in a somewhat fraught process, allocated quotas to the member states for their emissions, on a proposal from the Commission after consultation with each state, to a total estimated to keep the Union's emissions within the target. The emissions are carefully monitored and there are penalties for non-compliance. In 2005 the Union, in order to provide flexibility in the control of emissions, introduced its Emissions Trading Scheme (ETS), which allocates the rights among more than 5,000 of the Union's major industrial polluters, allowing those that emit less than their quotas to sell the unused rights to those that use more, and thus creating a 'carbon market' which determines the cost of carbon within the Union. Since the rights were evidently issued too generously for the period up to 2008, appropriately sharper cuts in quotas are to be made for the period 2008–12, raising the carbon price high enough to discourage excessive use. This is particularly important since the European Council decided in 2006, following the best scientific advice, that the Union must achieve a 60% cut by 2050, in line with the global target deemed necessary to avoid potentially catastrophic change; and since, as is shown in Chapter 10, the Union is leading the world in this field, it needs to maintain its own credibility.

The Union also faces a very big task in ensuring that new member states from Central and Eastern Europe, grossly polluted during the Soviet period, measure up to its environmental standards.

Long transitional periods of up to 11 years have been used before the newcomers are required to apply all the EU laws, and to keep some protection against unfair competition from those that are exonerated from costly obligations in the meantime. In addition, the Union has continued to provide financial support through the structural funds to ensure that the new member states can achieve the still dauntingly large task ahead of them.

Chapter 7

'An area of freedom, security and justice'

Ernest Bevin, the great Foreign Secretary in the first post-war Labour government, said that the aim of his foreign policy 'really was … to grapple with the whole problem of passports and visas', so that he could 'go down to Victoria Station', where trains departed for the Continent, 'get a railway ticket, and go where the Hell I liked without a passport or anything else'. The old trade unionist retained his vision of the brotherhood of man. But the foreign minister found himself defending the sovereignty of states; and he rejected the idea of British membership of the emergent Community, which was eventually to make the realization of his vision feasible.

Already in 1958 the Rome Treaty included 'persons', along with goods, services, and capital, in the four freedoms of movement across the frontiers between the member states. For 'persons' this was limited to the right to cross them for purposes of work. A quarter of a century later, the Single European Act defined the internal market as 'an area without internal frontiers'. Mrs Thatcher's government held that these words implied no change, because they were qualified by the addition 'in accordance with the Treaty', which in relevant respects still stood. But governments of the more federalist states intended to take the words literally: to abolish controls at their mutual borders and thus make movement across them free for all.

This idea was given legal expression in the Schengen Agreements of 1985 and 1990, Schengen being the small town in Luxembourg, symbolically alongside the frontiers with both France and Germany, where these three states, together with Belgium and the Netherlands, signed the agreements. The number of signatories has since grown until what has often been called Schengenland has been signed up to by all the EU states save Britain and Ireland, as well as Efta members.

Schengen had two main aims. The first concerned border controls: to eliminate those internal to Schengenland; establish controls round its external frontier; and set rules to deal with asylum, immigration, and the movement or residence of other countries' nationals within the area. The second was to cooperate in combating crime.

Cross-border criminal activity grows for reasons similar to those that drive cross-border economic activity: advancing technology, particularly in transport and communications. As with trade, cross-border cooperation is needed if the rule of law is to keep abreast of it. With the intense relationship engendered by their economic integration, the member states have a special need for such cooperation. A first step was taken in 1974 with the 'Trevi' agreement to exchange information about terrorism; and the ministers and officials involved soon found it useful to include other forms of crime. This was a precursor of Schengen, which forged closer cooperation among law enforcement agencies of the states that were ready to go further together, and which has led to an extensive 'acquis' of legal texts, applying to the very large majority of EU member states.

Maastricht and the third pillar

Cross-border aspects of crime and the movement of people affect all member states, not just those of Schengenland. It was agreed that the Maastricht Treaty should provide for cooperation in these fields. Terrorism, drugs, fraud, and 'other serious forms of crime' were listed in the Treaty, along with external border controls, asylum, immigration, and movement across the internal borders by nationals from states outside the Union. The member states' judicial, administrative, police, and customs authorities were to cooperate in order to deal with them.

Some states, such as Germany, wanted this to be done within the Community institutions, with the Commission, Court, and Parliament as well as the Council playing their normal parts. Others such as Britain, defending their sovereignty, wanted to exclude as far as possible the institutions other than the Council. The upshot was the new 'third pillar' for Cooperation in Justice and Home Affairs (CJHA), set up alongside the Community 'first pillar'. The institutions for the CJHA were intergovernmental, with the unanimity procedure in the Council, only consultative roles for the Parliament and Commission, and none at all for the Court. The policy instruments were to be joint positions and actions determined by the Council, and conventions ratified by all the member states. One of the conventions was to establish the new policing body, Europol.

Not surprisingly, given the requirement of unanimous agreement among the then 15 governments before a decision could be taken, there had not been much progress by the time the Amsterdam Treaty was negotiated. No convention had yet entered into force and action in other respects was slow. But concern about cross-border crime and illegal immigration continued to grow; and the Eastern enlargement, expected to bring new problems, was approaching. So most member states wanted a stronger system.

Amsterdam and the first pillar too

The Amsterdam Treaty affirmed the intention to establish what it rather grandly called 'an area of freedom, security and justice' (AFSJ). While conditions in the Union are, in a general sense, notably free, secure, and just when compared with almost all other parts of the world, the words are used in the treaty in a more specific sense: freedom refers to free movement across internal borders; security, to protection against cross-border crime; and justice, mainly to judicial cooperation in civil as well as criminal matters. It still remains to be seen whether it was wise to appropriate words that have such wide and noble significance for such particular ends. The answer may depend on how far and how soon they are achieved.

As regards *freedom* of movement, almost all the Schengen acquis has already been transferred from the third to the first pillar. Thus the right of people to move freely throughout Schengenland is guaranteed by the Community institutions, though some member states have had to restore border checks temporarily in order to deal with influxes from other member states of non-EU nationals with false visas. The external border controls are not yet satisfactory. Nor is the common policy on immigration and asylum complete. Nor will there be freedom of movement without border checks throughout the Union while Britain, Denmark, and Ireland retain their controls.

The removal of border controls within Schengenland is nevertheless a major achievement, as is the transfer of these competences to the Community, with the Court of Justice fulfilling its normal functions – except in the fields of internal security and law and order, which remain under the control of the member states. Since 2004, qualified majority voting, co-decision, and the Commission's sole right of initiative have applied in parts of this field, allowing for further integration of Schengen into the Community.

Determined to keep its border controls, Britain opted out of the Amsterdam Treaty's provisions on freedom of movement; and Ireland, enjoying open frontiers with the UK, had to do the same.

But both have the right to opt into specific measures, provided the other governments agree unanimously in each case. The British government has said it intends eventually to participate fully in the Schengen acquis, apart from the aspects relating to border controls, while Denmark, which had signed up to the Schengen Agreements, has opted out of their transfer into the Community.

As regards *security*, the fight against cross-border crime remains mainly in the intergovernmental third pillar, whose designation, since competence regarding free movement has been transferred to the Community, has been reduced to 'Police and Judicial Cooperation in Criminal Matters'. In line with ever-growing concern about crime, the Amsterdam Treaty extended the list to include trafficking in persons, offences against children, and corruption; and money-laundering, forging money, and 'cyber-crime' have been added since. The Nice Treaty gave the Commission a right of initiative in the pillar, further strengthening its integration into the Community.

Police cooperation has developed significantly, resulting for example in big seizures of drugs on their way to Britain. Europol has made a useful contribution, though it could not become fully operational until its convention was fully ratified by all member states in July 1999, over five years after the Maastricht Treaty had provided for it. While the third pillar remains predominantly intergovernmental, with the unanimity procedure prevailing in the Council, the Amsterdam Treaty did provide that conventions, when ratified by half the member states, would enter into force in those states. There is also a role for the Court of Justice, which was given authority to rule on the interpretation of Union laws and on disputes between member states or between them and the Commission.

However, it is in the field of counter-terrorism that most significant progress has been made. After the September 2001 attacks on the US, the Union quickly pushed to develop its own abilities to act. A European arrest warrant that had been in limbo for several years was agreed in 2002, alongside an action plan that targets aspects of the prevention and prosecution of terrorist acts, as well as coordinating responses by member states. While these failed to prevent the attacks in Madrid in May 2004 and London in July 2005, they have demonstrated that the Union does have a potential role to play in one of the most visible issues in the international system.

In order to give free movement and the fight against crime a lift in the Union's political priorities, the European Council held a special meeting on the subject at Tampere under Finnish Presidency in October 1999. It decided among other things to establish a high-level European Police College and a body called Eurojust, bringing together member states' prosecutors, magistrates, and police officers to cooperate in criminal investigation and prosecution.

In the narrow definition of *justice* as judicial cooperation, some specific steps have been taken for member states to assist each other in cross-border problems relating to the recognition and enforcement of judgments, though not much has been done about the rights of victims of crime. The path chosen by the Union has been one of mutual recognition, rather than harmonization; but there has been agreement on several joint policies, most notably the European arrest warrant, which address some of the problems of cross-border crime.

In a broader definition of the word, distributive justice has been an issue in this field since Germany, with a much larger number of asylum-seekers than other member states, wanted measures to share the cost. This resulted in the creation of a European asylum policy that has coordinated national policies and allowed for an improved management of the significant population flows of the past ten years.

In a yet broader sense of justice, the Amsterdam Treaty responded to criticism that the Union had emphasized restrictions on immigration and asylum at the expense of concern about the treatment of the human beings involved. In the face of widespread public backlash against them, the treaty provided for measures to safeguard their rights, together with action more generally to combat racism and xenophobia. Coupled to the 2000 Charter on Fundamental Rights, the Union has now articulated a fairly substantial human rights protection programme, although the degree to which it can enforce this remains moot.

What's in the name?

Freedom of movement within Schengenland is an almost complete reality. If Bevin were able to go to the Gare du Nord or the Gare de Lyon today, he could buy a ticket and go without a passport wherever he liked within Schengenland, though not, unfortunately, to Victoria Station.

It is far from certain, however, that police and judicial cooperation under the third pillar will deliver enough security from cross-border crime. Such crime continues to proliferate and it is doubtful whether the EU institutions as they stand at present are strong enough to win the battle against it. Judicial cooperation is good as far as it goes. But, again owing to institutional weaknesses, it does not yet go far enough.

The persisting divisions of competences between the first and third pillars, as well as the differential memberships of the EU and Schengenland, result in confused lines of control, limited scope for action and a system that few members of the public either know or understand. In many ways, the Area of Freedom, Security and Justice is a classic example of the Union's wider problem:

it is a potentially useful means for tackling problems that are beyond the scope of individual member states, but it is hampered by the political compromises, abstruse jargon, and occasionally counter-intuitive policies that result from trying to bring together such a large number of actors without adequate institutional reform.

Chapter 8

A great civilian power ... and more, or less?

The main motives for creating the Community were peace between France, Germany, and the other member states, and prosperity for their citizens. But while their mutual relationship was particularly intense, relations with their neighbours and with countries further afield were also very important; and the logic of subsidiarity, that the Community should have responsibility for what it can do better than the member states acting separately, began to be applied to external as well as internal affairs.

The Community's external relations were, in line with its powers, originally concentrated in the economic field. But there were from the outset also political aims. For Germany, bordering on the Soviet bloc and with East Germany under Soviet control, the priority was solidarity in resistance to Soviet pressure. The French had a broader vision of the Community as a power in the world. Relations with the United States were a central element: for Monnet, in the form of a partnership between the Community and the US; for de Gaulle, to defy American hegemony. Monnet's view was widely shared and the Community came to be seen as a potential 'great civilian power'.

Many in France went beyond this, envisaging a Europe that could challenge American dominance in the field of defence. In other countries this view was generally resisted. But cooperation in foreign policy evolved to the point where the Union gave it the name 'Common Foreign and Security Policy'; and Britain, which had long been adamantly opposed to common action by the EU on defence, in 1999 joined France in initiating a modest EU defence capacity. This is still a minor, though increasingly significant, element in the Union's external relations. The Community's external economic policies remain much more important.

Meanwhile, the world has been becoming a more dangerous place, with sources of instability such as climate change, environmental degradation, cross-border crime, poverty, consequent mass migration, and terrorism, alongside the military forms of insecurity. The relative simplicity of the confrontation between the United States and the Soviet Union has been replaced by unrivalled American supremacy, and with the perspective of an emergent multipolar world in which the US is in the process of being joined by China and, probably later, India as giant powers, while Russia along with other, rising powers must also be taken into account; and the balance of bipolar economic power, with the predominance of the US and the EU, is being rapidly transformed, likewise with China and India as emergent giants, into a multipolar world economy. This is the world in which the EU has to find its place; and as the impact of the Iraq War of 2003 and the prolonged Doha Round of trade negotiations, together with surges of imports from China, have demonstrated, it is no simple task.

Europeans have generally reached a stage in their history, and particularly in the experience of living peaceably together in the EU, when they greatly value security and predictability in the relations among states, hence favour the creation of a secure multilateral system in the world. While the Union's military capabilities play a growing part in functions such as peacekeeping, its external economic, aid, and environmental policies, together with its experience in developing peaceful relations among states, have a major potential for contributing to both its own security and prosperity, and those in the wider world. In this perspective, much can be learned from the Union's experience so far. So we examine in this chapter why and how its structures for dealing with the rest of the world have been established; in Chapter 9, how it has come to be enlarged from 15 states in Western Europe to include most other European states; and in Chapter 10 how its policies for dealing with the rest of the world have been developed.

External economic relations

The Rome Treaty gave the Community its common external tariff as an instrument for trade policy, called in the jargon 'common commercial policy'. This was not a foregone conclusion. Some wanted the member states to keep their existing tariffs, below the average in Germany and Benelux, higher in France and Italy. But the French insisted on the common tariff, partly because they feared competition from cheap imports seeping through the low-tariff states, but partly also because they wanted the Community to have an instrument with which it could start to become a force in world affairs.

This has remained a persistent French theme. It was one of the motives for the drive towards the single currency, challenging the hegemony of the dollar; and it has continued with the effort to build a European defence capacity, for which the term 'Europe puissance' has been coined, contrasted with a mere European 'space' preoccupied with business affairs. Neither those French who were highly protectionist, nor the British who at that time criticized the common tariff as a protectionist device, envisaged that it would in fact be the trigger for the Kennedy Round of tariff cuts, which was the first step towards the Community's role as the foremost promoter of world trade liberalization, and thus also towards demonstrating the power of a common instrument of external policy.

That power has been shown in the field of agriculture too, with much less fortunate results. The system of import levies and export subsidies has been used in a highly protectionist way, to the detriment of the Community's consumers and international trade relations, including its own industrial exports. But the external trade policy, taken as a whole, has been of considerable benefit both to its citizens and to international trade.

External trade relations are conducted effectively by the Community institutions. Policies are decided and trade agreements approved by the Council under the procedure of qualified majority; negotiations are conducted by the Commission within the policy mandate thus decided, and in consultation with a special committee appointed by the Council; and the Court has jurisdiction on points of law. Parliaments do not usually play much part in relation to trade negotiations, apart from formally approving the results. But the Treaties did not even provide for consultation of the European Parliament about matters of trade policy, though it is accorded the right to give or withhold its assent over treaties of association and, more importantly, of accession, although the Parliament does play a significant part in external relations more generally.

When the Rome Treaty was drafted, trade in goods was all-important; trade in services was of little account, and was not mentioned in the chapter on the common commercial policy. But services now comprise about one-third of all world trade. Yet despite the success of the normal Community system as it applies to the trade in goods, trade in services has remained subject to more intergovernmental procedures. While the momentum of successful negotiations on trade in goods has carried the Community through a series of trade rounds, these procedures could still weaken its capacity to negotiate effectively on services. So the Nice Treaty applied qualified majority voting to trade in all services save in the fields of culture, audio-visual services, education, health and social services, and some transport services.

Shares of world trade of EU, US, China, Japan, and others, 2004

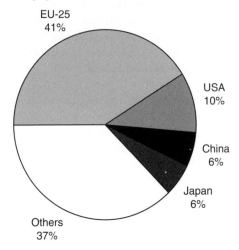

Exports

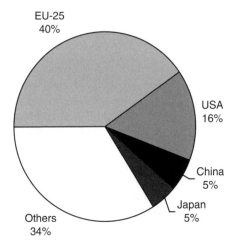

Imports

Development aid has also become a major instrument of the Union's external policy, initiated, likewise on French insistence, with the Rome Treaty's provision for a fund for the then colonies of member states. This has since burgeoned so that the Union provides aid for countries throughout the less-developed parts of the world. Thus the EU, together with its member states, has become by far the world's largest source of aid; and within Europe the Union's instruments of trade and aid policy, along with the prospect of membership, have been a major external influence favouring the successful transformation of the new member states from Central and Eastern Europe. It was indeed fortunate that France insisted on the original grant of instruments for the Community's external policy.

The environment too, and climate change in particular, has become a major field for international negotiation; and though the Union's external policy remains subject to a somewhat more intergovernmental procedure than its trade policy, the EU has nonetheless, as we shall see in Chapter 10, had a decisive impact on negotiations to counter global warming and destruction of the ozone layer.

Despite the introduction of the euro, the EU does not yet play a similar part in the international monetary system. The institutional arrangements for conducting an external monetary policy are not at present strong enough to enable it to exert its potential weight in this very important field.

Foreign policy

Cooperation in foreign policy among the member states was introduced in 1970 as an element of deepening along with the widening to include Britain, Ireland, and Denmark. The name given to this activity was European Political Cooperation (EPC): the word 'political' being used by ministries of foreign affairs, distinguishing what they saw as 'high politics' from such matters as economics, evidently regarded as low. But the Community's external economic policies were already a great deal more important than anything the EPC was to achieve during the following years, particularly as France, in the early years after de Gaulle, insisted that the EPC be kept not only intergovernmental but also rigorously separate from the Community.

The EPC did achieve an important early result when the member states got human rights placed on the agenda of the Conference on Security and Cooperation in Europe. The Soviet Union accepted the text that was finally adopted, which though nobody then thought it of much consequence, in the event gave support to the agitation that contributed to the dissolution of the Soviet bloc. More generally, the member states' diplomats developed ways of working together that were to produce many joint positions on a wide range of subjects, both in relations with other states and in the United Nations. By 1985 France was ready to accept that the EPC should come closer to the Community and it was included in the Single European Act.

The next formal development of foreign policy cooperation was its incorporation in the Maastricht Treaty alongside the Community, as the 'second pillar' of the EU. The prospect of German unification had alarmed the French, who feared that the larger Germany might downgrade the Franco-German partnership and pursue an autonomous Eastern policy. Just as they promoted the single currency to anchor Germany in the Community, so they wanted a common foreign policy to limit German autonomy in relations with the East; the Germans, far from opposing this, saw it as part of the design for a Europe united on federal lines; and both President Mitterrand and Chancellor Kohl saw a common foreign policy together with the single currency as cementing permanent peace in Europe. So they proposed the IGC on 'political union' to run in parallel with the one on economic and monetary union.

15. Kohl and Mitterrand hold hands among cemeteries where a million French and German soldiers are buried

When Mrs Thatcher asked them what they meant by political union, she got no clear answer. One reason was that, while both were agreed on the idea of a common foreign policy, which was one of the two specific things to which the term was applied, they disagreed about reform of the institutions, which was the other. For while the French wanted to strengthen the intergovernmental elements, in particular the European Council, the Germans wanted to move towards a federal system by strengthening the Parliament. So they could hardly speak with one voice about it. Thatcher wanted neither and, though she accepted the existing EPC, did not want the Community institutions to have a hand in it. While Germany envisaged that foreign policy would move towards becoming a Community competence, France too opposed the idea; and the outcome was the intergovernmental 'second pillar' for a Common Foreign and Security Policy (CFSP).

The CFSP was given a grander name than the EPC and more elaborate institutions. Following Europe's poor showing in the

Gulf War, defence was mentioned in the treaty, but in ambiguous terms to accommodate both the French desire for an autonomous European defence capacity and British opposition to any such thing, for fear it could weaken Nato. So nothing much resulted from the use of the word defence. Nor indeed did the CFSP then produce notably better results than the EPC had done before. So there was a second try, in the Amsterdam Treaty, to devise a satisfactory second pillar.

That Treaty set very general objectives for the CFSP, ranging from international cooperation to support for democracy, the rule of law, and human rights. In an attempt to make the Union more decisive, there was provision for voting by qualified majority. But this was hedged about by rights of opting out and veto. Thus there can be QMV on common positions and joint actions, but only if taken 'on the basis of a common strategy', which has to be adopted unanimously; and that can narrow the scope for decisions taken by QMV as much as a member state government may desire. Governments can also refer decisions they oppose to the European Council, where again they can apply the veto; and they can opt out of decisions when they wish to do so. The Nice Treaty expanded somewhat the opening for 'enhanced cooperation' among a group of member states, with some scope for QMV, though not where there are defence implications. This has not been used so far, but could become more important in the future if some states become frustrated by the reluctance of others.

This complexity reflects the reality that where actions depend on the instruments that belong to member states, not the Union, they are likely to be applied with varying degrees of commitment by governments that have what appear to them to be significant objections. But a majority decision to act will be properly applied if it depends on the use of an instrument that belongs to the Union. Such instruments can be fiscal, such as the common external tariff, or financial, such as aid and assistance, or monetary, such as the euro; and the Union does dispose of these. An instrument can also be a legal act such as an association agreement, where QMV does not up to the time of writing apply. The Union also, with the rapid reaction force and battle groups, is building instruments in the field of defence. But sending soldiers on missions where they may be killed is seen as too sensitive a matter to be decided by the Union against the wishes of the state of which they are citizens. So majority voting is excluded from the field of defence. But apart from this, the limits to how far QMV can be of practical use, without opting out or unanimity in the background, are set by the extent to which the Union is given common instruments that can be used to carry out the decisions.

This attempt to insert an element of majority voting into the CFSP did not itself lead to much more decisive common action. But one of the other changes introduced by the Amsterdam Treaty has had a more substantial impact: the appointment of a 'High Representative', who is at the same time Secretary General of the Council Secretariat, to contribute to the making and implementation of foreign policy decisions and to 'assist' the Council's President-in-Office in representing the Union in the field of CFSP. Javier Solana was given this position, and also that of Secretary General of Western European Union (WEU). Combining these three posts, and with his track record as a successful Secretary General of Nato, he has significantly influenced the decisions and actions of the CFSP.

It is, however, the Community institutions that control the instruments of external economic policy; and here the President of the Commission, and the Commissioners for fields such as trade policy, aid, environment, and enlargement negotiations, have major responsibilities. The part that the treaty gives the Commission to play in the making of common foreign and security policy, of merely submitting proposals when requested by the Council to do so, fails to recognize this reality.

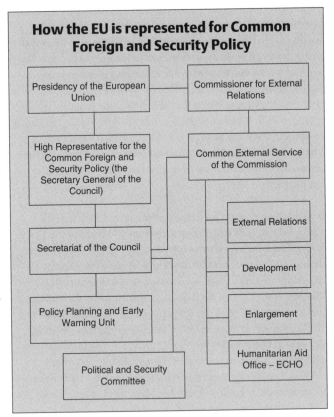

How the EU is represented for Common Foreign and Security Policy

Presidency of the European Union	Commissioner for External Relations

High Representative for the Common Foreign and Security Policy (the Secretary General of the Council)	Common External Service of the Commission

External Relations

Secretariat of the Council	

Development

Enlargement

Policy Planning and Early Warning Unit	

Humanitarian Aid Office – ECHO

Political and Security Committee

A policy planning unit was also established in the Council Secretariat, drawing staff from the Secretariat itself, the member states, WEU, and the Commission, to prepare thinking on CFSP issues likely to arise. The Parliament too became involved in the foreign policy process through the inclusion of CFSP expenditure in the part of the Community budget over which it shares control with the Council. But this does not apply for military or defence operations or 'where the Council unanimously decides otherwise'.

A defect of these arrangements is that substantial sums of money for CFSP purposes can, as crises in the Balkans have shown, be needed urgently, whereas the budgetary arrangements for the CFSP are not adapted to putting up such money fast; and this is a serious defect, because while such funds are awaited, crises can spin out of control.

Security

Awareness that the Union should provide more effective military backing for its common policy in former Yugoslavia spurred governments to strengthen its capacity in the field of defence. While recognizing that they depend on Nato and the US for defence against any major threat to their security, they used somewhat stronger language on the Union's own capacity in the Amsterdam Treaty than at Maastricht, envisaging 'the progressive framing of a common defence policy, which might lead to a common defence', the immediate purpose of which was to include humanitarian tasks, peacekeeping, and 'crisis management, including peacemaking'. More directly significant than aspirations expressed in the treaties, however, are the arrangements for putting them into effect; and instead of leaving it to the slow and difficult process of an IGC to turn the aspiration of a common defence capacity into a fact, the treaty gave the European Council the power to do so by a unanimous vote.

The war over Kosovo had demonstrated that Europeans, though their defence expenditure amounted to two-thirds that of the Americans, were capable of delivering only one-tenth of the firepower; and their influence over the conduct of the action was correspondingly limited. This brought together the British and French, who had made the principal European contribution, to launch their defence initiative. Experience in the Gulf and the Balkan wars had shown the French that they had to come closer to Nato if they were to make an effective military contribution, while the British for their part had come to see the merit of working with the French; and, having declined to become a founder member of the eurozone, the government saw defence as a field in which a central role for Britain in the Union could be secured.

The result was the joint proposal for an EU rapid reaction force 'up to' 50,000–60,000 strong, which was adopted by the European Council in Helsinki in December 1999; and it was agreed to integrate WEU into the Union. The EU began to develop its European Security and Defence Policy (ESDP) as the security arm of the CFSP. It established an EU defence planning and staff structure, with Council meetings in which defence ministers participate along with the foreign ministers, a Military Committee representing member states' 'defence chiefs', and military staff within the Council Secretariat; and it converted the Political Committee, responsible to the Council, into a Political and Security Committee. Preparations proceeded for establishing the rapid reaction force, to undertake peacekeeping and crisis management autonomously 'where Nato as a whole is not engaged', though Nato, which in practice meant American, facilities such as air transport and satellite-based intelligence would usually be required; and this means American consent to any substantial operations. Thus the British government's fears about weakening Nato have been allayed; and all member states, including Austria, Finland, Ireland, and Sweden, with their traditions of neutrality, were reassured by the provisions that any member state can opt out of, or into, any action.

This illustrates the difficulties confronting the Union's defence capacity. A critical mass of member states must agree to an action before it can be undertaken; for substantial operations that require Nato facilities and hence American consent, the Americans may not agree to what Europeans want to do, which would give rise to tensions within Nato; and where a European critical mass and American agreement are both available, the intergovernmental arrangements may be too weak to devise and manage a successful operation. While Nato's system is also intergovernmental, American hegemonial leadership has caused it to work. There is no hegemon among the member states; and while this makes it more feasible to develop the Union as a working democracy, it will at the same time make an intergovernmental system in the field of defence hard to operate.

The Union's development in a field so sensitive for sovereignty can hardly be expected to run smoothly. But it encountered rougher waters following al-Qaeda's terrorist attack on the United States in September 2001, when relationships between states were disrupted both in Nato and within the Union itself. The Americans adopted a more unilateralist approach, with the 'war on terror', accompanied by the intervention in Iraq in March 2003; and the Union's member states were sharply divided, with the British, Italian, Polish, and Spanish governments leading the support for the American intervention, while the French and Germans, shortly to be joined by the Italians and Spaniards after changes of government, led those against it. This might have been expected to obstruct the continued development of the Union's capacity in the field of military security as well as relationships within Nato; and it did delay progress of the ESDP for a while. But the Union continued to develop its capacity in the field of security and by 2004 was able to replace Nato's peacekeeping force in Bosnia, to establish the European Defence Agency (EDA) in order to improve the efficiency of arms production, and to decide on a programme to create a set of battle groups, each 1,500 strong, which are intended to be deployable within five days of a Council decision to launch an operation. In 2007, the mandate for the IGC on the Reform Treaty provided that, in addition to strengthening the role of the High Representative, a group of member states with the necessary military capability may establish permanent structured cooperation within the Union in the field of defence.

As the Union develops its capacity in the field of security, it will become something more than a great civilian power. But its strength in the economic, environmental, and other aspects of external policy, somewhat condescendingly called 'soft power', is already very important, and has great further potential as a force for the development of a safer and more prosperous world.

Chapter 9
The EU and the rest of Europe

A most impressive aspect of the European Community project has been its ability to develop and expand from a small group of relatively similar states in Western Europe into a European Union of much greater width and depth. The process of deepening and widening since the 1950s, with its synergies and contradictions, has been recounted in Chapter 2. Within this long process of enlargement, it is the expansion into Central and Eastern Europe that has, apart from de Gaulle's reaction to the British application, been the most contentious. While member states generally agreed that Eastern enlargement was to be welcomed, to extend the area of prosperity and security, there have also been greatly varying degrees of enthusiasm, to the point where discussion of 'enlargement fatigue' became not uncommon in the old member states. Certainly, there have been problems on the way, but enlargement can be seen as an essential part of the EU and its continued development, not least in its dealings with those who remain outside; and the treaty still affirms that membership is open to any European state that respects 'the principles of liberty, democracy, respect for human rights and fundamental freedoms, and the rule of law'.

Enlargement to almost all of Western Europe

There is a routine for the process of enlargement. When an application is received, the Council asks the Commission for its 'Opinion', on the basis of which the Council may, unanimously, approve a mandate for negotiations. The Commission negotiates, supervised by the Council; and an eventual treaty of accession has to be adopted by unanimity in the Council and with the assent of the Parliament, followed by ratification in all the member states.

Membership can be preceded by a form of association. The original example was the Treaty of Association between Greece and the Community in 1962, which provided for the removal of trade barriers over a transitional period, various forms of cooperation, and a Council of Association. It also envisaged eventual membership; and after various vicissitudes, Greece did indeed become a member in 1981.

Portugal and Spain were not eligible for association in the 1960s. Their regimes were incompatible with the Community, for which only democratic countries were suitable partners; and Portugal had already in 1960 become a founder member of the European Free Trade Association (Efta), which Britain had promoted in reaction to the establishment of the EEC and which, being confined to a purely trading relationship, was not so concerned about the political complexion of its members. So when democracy replaced dictatorship in the 1970s, both Iberian countries negotiated entry to the Community without any prior form of association. This was one reason why the negotiations were protracted, with entry achieved only in 1986. Protectionist resistance, from French farmers in particular, was, however, more significant.

The path to membership was different for the more northerly members of Efta. The British, Danes, Norwegians, Swedes, and

Swiss had eschewed the political implications of Community membership; and the Austrians were precluded by their peace treaty. Britain, Denmark, and Ireland joined in 1973 without having been associated in any way. Bilateral free trade agreements were at the same time concluded between the Community and each of the other Efta states, which by then included Iceland; and they were later signed with Finland, which joined in 1986, and Liechtenstein, in 1991.

As soon as the Soviet constraint was removed in 1989, Austria applied for EC membership. Finland, Norway, Sweden, and Switzerland were not far behind. Delors, hoping to delay such enlargement lest it dilute the Community, devised a proposal for a European Economic Area (EEA) to include the Efta countries with the EC in an extended single market. But the governments of those five did not want to be excluded from decision-taking in the Community, so they all applied for membership, which Austria, Finland, and Sweden achieved in 1995, after a short negotiation facilitated by their existing free trade relationship. Norwegians rejected accession in their referendum and Swiss voters refused to accept even the EEA. So Switzerland continues with its bilateral free trade agreement and only a vestigial EEA remains, associating Norway, Iceland, and Liechtenstein with the Union.

Enlargement to the East

Throughout the cold war, relations were cool between the EC and the Soviet Union. The Soviet Union refused to accord the Community legal recognition, seeing it as strengthening the 'capitalist camp'; and the Community refused to negotiate with Comecon, the economic organization dominated by the Soviet Union. Following 1989, and the dissolution of the Soviet bloc, the Central and East European countries turned towards the Community, which they saw as a bastion of prosperity, democracy, and protection from a chaotic (and collapsing) Soviet Union. They naturally envisaged membership.

16. The Berlin Wall comes down

The simplest case was the German Democratic Republic, as the Soviet-controlled part of Germany had called itself. The GDR became part of the Federal Republic of Germany in 1990; and the Community made the necessary technical adjustments at speed so that the enlarged Germany could assume the German membership without delay.

For the other countries of Central and Eastern Europe, extensive aid and development packages were put together under the Commission's leadership. Projects such as PHARE sought to provide assistance with economic and political restructuring for the emergent democracies, spending roughly €600 million per year between 1990 and 2003, when it was wound up. However, such assistance, while welcome, was seen by many in the region as a diversion from membership. Indeed, such a view was an accurate reflection of the ambivalence felt by many of the Union's members about enlargement. While publicly proclaiming the historic mission of the Union to reunite Europe peacefully, many politicians were concerned about the admission of a large number of relatively poor, relatively small, and relatively unstable new members, whose populations might move en masse to the West to find employment.

It was only in 1993, at the Copenhagen European Council, that the Union agreed the principle of offering full membership to those who wanted it. However, the Union also agreed for the first time to expand on the provisions of the treaty and laid out what became known as the Copenhagen criteria: stable democracy, human rights and protection of minorities, the rule of law, a competitive market economy, and 'ability to take on the obligations of membership including adherence to the aims of political, economic and monetary union'. While political union meant different things in different member states, the significance of 'the obligations of membership' was clear enough, including the huge task of applying not far short of 100,000 pages of legislation, mostly concerning the single market. To allay fears that widening would result in weakening, there was also the condition that the Union should have 'the capacity to absorb new members while maintaining the momentum of integration'.

Despite this laying out of the threshold for membership, and the development of extensive programmes of assistance to the states of Central and Eastern Europe in order to help meet them, it was only after the conclusion of the Amsterdam Treaty in 1997 that things really started to move. In 1998, the Union judged that a first wave of five had made the necessary progress, so negotiations began in 1998 with the Czech Republic, Estonia, Hungary, Poland, and Slovenia, as well as Cyprus, which had also applied to join; and, in 2000, also with a second wave comprising Bulgaria, Latvia, Lithuania, Romania, and Slovakia, as well as Malta. While the Union had indicated that each individual accession negotiation would proceed at its own speed, it was agreed at the 2003 Copenhagen European Council that all save Bulgaria and

Map 2 Applicants for accession

Current member states

Candidate countries
(Croatia, Macedonia, Turkey)

Potential candidate countries
(Albania, Bosnia and Herzegovina,
Montenegro, Serbia (including Kosovo))

Romania would be able to join in May 2004. These two were able to become members in 2007.

The process of enlargement to the East was very protracted, for a number of reasons. On the part of the new member states, the adjustments required were very substantial, especially within the context of emerging from Communist, planned economy systems. Many states simply lacked the institutions, resources, or experience necessary to implement fundamental changes in the operation of many areas of public policy and decision-making. On the part of the existing member states, we have already mentioned the fears about the increased heterogeneity of the Union and implications of free movement and of the state of EU policies. This last point was to take up much of the Union's time in the late 1990s, as it struggled to reform CAP and cohesion policies to cope with the imminent arrival of a large number of poor states with significant agricultural sectors: those reforms are discussed in Chapter 5. Seen broadly, the solution that was found was to reform the policies by changing the types of support provided, but also to limit the amount that new states could claim in any case. Such an apparently unfair approach to new members has been a consistent feature of all previous enlargements, as existing members seek to protect their interests while they can and while an applicant state has little leverage to fight it. This was also evident with the discussions about institutional reform that culminated in the Nice Treaty, which a number of member states found unsatisfactory enough to call for the constitutional Convention.

For all of this concern, perhaps the most remarkable feature of the post-enlargement EU is how unproblematic it has been to date. Despite the failure to replace the Nice settlement with the Constitutional Treaty, the Union's decision-making bodies have functioned without undue problems arising from the enlargement and the gridlock that some had predicted in the 1990s has not come to pass. Indeed, when we consider the most obvious crises within the Union, these have been more about old member states than new ones: the French and Dutch 'no' votes on the Constitutional Treaty; the Anglo-French split over the Iraq War and its aftermath. Partly this has been because the new members have kept a low profile as they learn the ropes of how to work within the Union, with Poland something of an exception; but it is also partly driven by the depth of structural adjustment that these states have made to become members: several of them have been more compliant with the requirements of membership than those they have joined.

South Eastern Europe

South Eastern Europe denotes mainly the states of former Yugoslavia: Croatia, Bosnia-Hercegovina, Macedonia, Montenegro, and Serbia, of which Kosovo remained formally a province. Albania is also included within the term, but in current discussions of EU policy Slovenia is not since, though it was also one of the former Yugoslav republics, it has qualified to become a member state.

Before it disintegrated, the former Yugoslavia had been closer to the Community than any other Central or East European state. Then came the disintegration and the wars. The United States initially wanted the Europeans to deal with the problems. Jacques Poos, Luxembourg's Foreign Minister and President-in-Office of the Council in the first half of 1991, famously said 'This is the hour of Europe'. Not having a significant Serb minority, Slovenia secured independence without much fighting. But bitter wars ensued in Croatia, Bosnia, and later in Kosovo, and in all three cases the Union failed completely to match Poos's claim. Instead, it was the US and Nato that were the main actors in securing a durable peace settlement in the region, the EU being relegated to providing humanitarian relief.

The key consequence of this for the Union was to stimulate a complete review of the Common Foreign and Security Policy, most notably with the creation of hard military capabilities in order to secure the so-called Petersberg tasks of humanitarian relief, peacekeeping, and crisis management. It also helped to make the Union consider how its various external policies linked up together, most obviously seen in the creation of the High Representative to give a single face to the EU's work. As far as the Balkans were concerned, the result of the EU's initial failure was a return to the drawing board and the production of a Stability Pact for South-East Europe. This overarching set of policies, designed to strengthen democracy, human rights, and economic reform, was later followed by Stability and Association Agreements between the Union and each of the West Balkan states save, so far, Serbia. This is backed by the Union's Instrument for Pre-Accession Assistance, which provides some €500 million per year for the West Balkans. With the slow stabilization of the region, the Union has been able to offer full candidate status to Macedonia and a provisional status to the others with Stability and Association Agreements, thus providing a strong incentive for local politicians to follow the example of the other Central and East Europeans.

Russia and the CIS

The three Baltic republics of the former Soviet Union, Estonia, Latvia, and Lithuania, declined to join Russia in the successor Commonwealth of Independent States (CIS) and became EU members in 2004. Among the states that stayed with the CIS, six can claim to be European: Armenia, Belarus, Georgia, Moldova, Ukraine, and Russia itself. They could therefore, if they come to fulfil the conditions of stable democracy and competitive market economy, apply for membership of the Union.

As the EU has enlarged itself to the borders of Russia and Ukraine, the question of enlargement to CIS states has been

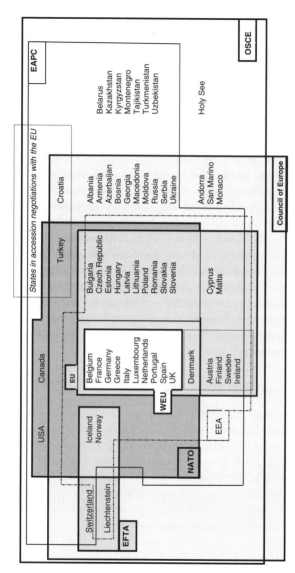

Map 3 The architecture of Europe, 2007

EAPC

OSCE

States in accession negotiations with the EU

Council of Europe

Croatia

Belarus
Kazakhstan
Kyrgyzstan
Montenegro
Tajikistan
Turkmenistan
Uzbekistan

Holy See

Albania
Armenia
Azerbaijan
Bosnia
Georgia
Macedonia
Moldova
Russia
Serbia
Ukraine

Andorra
San Marino
Monaco

Turkey

USA

Canada

Bulgaria
Czech Republic
Estonia
Hungary
Latvia
Lithuania
Poland
Romania
Slovakia
Slovenia

Cyprus
Malta

Iceland
Norway

EU

Belgium
France
Germany
Greece
Italy
Luxembourg
Netherlands
Portugal
Spain
UK

Denmark

Austria
Finland
Sweden
Ireland

WEU

Switzerland
Liechtenstein

EFTA

NATO

EEA

raised. The size of Russia, however, combined with the much greater economic and political disparities with the EU than those found in Central and Eastern Europe, stand in the way. The policy has therefore been to develop closer bilateral and multilateral relations rather than to envisage membership. The other states too face great difficulties. But although Ukraine faces major problems in becoming a stable democracy, the desire for membership is not, in the long term, unrealistic.

The EU has, however, long been eager to help with the transition to democracy and free-market economics throughout the CIS. From 1991 until 2007, the Union operated a very extensive programme of assistance known as Technical Assistance to the Commonwealth of Independent States (TACIS). With a budget of around €500 million a year, TACIS concentrated on such things as enterprise restructuring and development, administrative reform, social services, education, and, as the biggest item, nuclear safety, which accounts for a large part of the regional programmes. As will be seen in Chapter 10, TACIS has been superseded by the European Neighbourhood Policy.

The Union's relationship with Russia remains an ambiguous one. While the military rivalry of the cold war has largely gone, the uncertain nature of Russian democracy under Vladimir

CIS states with EU agreements

The EU has Partnership and Cooperation Agreements with:

Armenia	Kazakhstan	Russian Federation
Azerbaijan	Kyrgyzstan	Ukraine
Georgia	Moldova	Uzbekistan

Putin in the new century has created new points of tension. As Russia's military might has faded and the shift to free-market economics has not yet been as successful as hoped, so the Russian government has started to use its massive natural energy exports to Europe as a new way of being a player on the international scene. The 2000s have seen repeated instances of state-controlled gas and oil companies using their size and privileged relationship with the Kremlin to gain increasingly dominant positions within EU energy markets, helped by the EU's own energy liberalization agenda. While this dominance is conditioned by the fact that Russian companies are now dependent upon European markets for much of their profits, until there is more confidence in the political and legal systems in Russia, the Union is not likely to seek to develop its relationship beyond the current Partnership and Cooperation Agreement.

Turkey

We cannot complete this chapter without reference to Turkey. If Russia is a problematic partner for the EU, then Turkey has been more like a thorn in its side, because it has so openly and heartily wished to become a member of the Union for such a long time.

Turkey concluded a Treaty of Association with the EEC in 1964, which was like that of Greece, save that the Community's doubts about Turkey were reflected in a transition period of 22 years and no clear commitment to membership. Turkey lodged its application for membership in 1987, but it was not until 1999 that the Union recognized it as a candidate, and negotiations began only in 2005, with accession not expected before 2015. Even by the EU's low standards, such a protracted process requires some explanation.

Union politicians have voiced a number of reasons for doubting whether Turkey should become a member. First, there has been reference to the Copenhagen criteria and the country's unsuitability on the grounds of human rights abuses, the role of the military in politics, weaknesses in the economy, and the extent to which reforms can meaningfully be made. Second, there are concerns regarding the size of Turkey (it would before long be the EU's largest member state, owing to its high birth rate) and the resultant potential for large-scale migration to other member states and for-voting weight in the Council. Third, there has been much talk of 'enlargement fatigue' and the need for a more substantial pause before such a major expansion. Fourth, and perhaps underlining all of these other dimensions, is the notion of Turkey's 'otherness'. As a majority Muslim population, as a state with a tenuous claim to be geographically 'European', and as a state with a very different historical path from that of current members, it challenges many conceptions of what the EU is and should be.

For the Turks' part, their persistence in the face of such opposition reflects the strength of the Western Kemalist project in the country and of its self-conception as a bridge between East and West. Certainly, successive Turkish governments have made very extensive modifications to legal and political structures in order to secure the accession negotiations that they so desired, something that is all the more surprising for the lack of certainty that such negotiations would occur. However, Turkish patience, especially in the general public, is not infinite, and in recent years there has been a cooling in the desire to join the Union. Again, this is a standard feature of enlargements: as membership draws closer, people begin to see the costs as well as the benefits.

None the less, Turkey's membership remains unresolved. Bowing to public pressure, both Austria and France recently introduced new procedures that require referendums on the accession of any new member state, which would be highly unlikely to give Turkey membership. However, the question has to be asked of whether or not excluding Turkey is desirable.

The EU already has over 15 million Muslims, so religion is not the barrier that some imagine. Likewise, admitting Turkey could help consolidate the EU's status as a global power, both through the admission of a state that bridges into the Middle East and through its extensive military capability. Whatever decision is finally made, it will have serious implications for the Union and its future development.

Chapter 10
The EU in the world

Having shown how 'federal institutions can unite highly developed states', the Community might serve as an example of how 'to create a more prosperous and peaceful world'. Such was the hope that Jean Monnet expressed in 1954 to the students of Columbia University in New York. The EU has been concerned, like others, to look after its own interests, even if it is often hard to reach agreement on what these are. But Europeans have become more aware than most others that these do include the creation of a prosperous and peaceful world. How do its actions, as distinct from its example as a region of peace and welfare, contribute to that end?

The Community as a great trading power

The United States sponsored the uniting of Europe, from Marshall Aid to the birth and early development of the Community. Monnet reciprocated with the idea of an increasingly equal EC–US partnership. Soon after the EEC was founded with its common external tariff, the US responded by initiating the Kennedy Round of trade liberalization in the Gatt; and this led in 1967, after five years of laborious negotiations, to the agreement to cut tariffs by one-third.

That would have been out of the question had the Community not become, with its common tariff as an instrument of external policy, a trading partner on level terms with the US. As an observer in Washington put it, the EC was 'now the most important member of Gatt', and the key to further efforts to liberalize trade. So it indeed became in later rounds of Gatt negotiations, as the creative American impulse of the post-war period declined. The Community played the leading part in the Uruguay Round, concluded in 1994. With tariffs on most manufactures already low, the focus moved to non-tariff barriers where the single market programme gave the Community a unique experience in techniques of liberalization. Its experience was also relevant to the replacement of the Gatt by the World Trade Organization, with its wider scope and greater powers for resolving disputes: a step, perhaps, towards validating the suggestion that the EC's 'example of effective international law-making' might at some stage be 'replicated at global level'.

Of course the Community's trade relations have engendered the normal clash of interests, or at least of what participants suppose to be their interests, with agriculture the prime bone of contention. The protectionist common agricultural policy damaged trading partners such as Australia, Canada, New Zealand, and the US. Following UK accession, this was particularly harmful to the first three which, under the system of Commonwealth preference, had enjoyed free entry for their exports to Britain and then, with a few exceptions such as a quota for New Zealand butter, faced the full rigour of the Community's agricultural protection: a blow that could have been avoided had Britain not failed to join when the Rome Treaty was negotiated. It was not until the 1990s that the Community began to carry out serious reform, when it cut the level of protection for some major items by about half; and it was agreed in the Uruguay Round that the trade-disrupting export subsidies would be eliminated in the following round: a tough challenge for both the Community and the United States.

While moving closer together on agriculture, the Community and the US diverged over environmental, cultural, and consumer protection issues, with the Europeans favouring standards which led to restriction of their imports from the US and which the Americans regarded as protectionist. Genetically modified organisms, hormone-treated beef, noisy aero-engines, data privacy, and films and television programmes were cases in point.

The friction induced by the Community's network of preferential arrangements has, on the contrary, been eased as tariffs were reduced in successive Gatt rounds. That network had become so extensive, covering almost the whole of Europe and the less-developed countries, that only a few remained outside it, including Australia, Canada, Japan, New Zealand, South Africa, and the US. The Americans were irked by the EC's preferences for particular countries. But the other side of this coin was the relationships that the EC established with large parts of the world's South, which were, however, put to a hard test in the Doha Round of trade negotiations that opened in 2001, following a fractious prelude in Seattle, with anti-globalization riots in the streets and contention in the conference between the EU, wanting a comprehensive agenda, and the US, preferring to concentrate on fields such as agriculture and the environment.

The Union's desire to include matters such as investment, competition policy, public procurement, and trade facilitation, known as the 'Singapore issues', was motivated partly by the view that the world should start moving, as the EU itself had done, beyond the focus on tariffs and import quotas in order to deal with other areas of policy that have a growing impact on trade. But developing countries were not ready for this; and their negotiating power was enhanced by the creation of the G20, led by Brazil,

China, India, and South Africa, with others representing regional and trading interests. Agriculture also emerged, as usual, as an obstacle, with the European and American farm lobbies resisting liberalization; and for some less-developed countries there was an additional problem arising from the Union's 'everything but arms' decision to abolish restrictions on imports from the 40 poorest countries, to the detriment of their competitors in other less-developed countries.

By May 2004 the Trade Commissioner, Pascal Lamy, was able to offer to reduce the Union's insistence on the Singapore issues and to negotiate the removal of all export subsidies, thus enabling the negotiations to move forward in that year. At the same time a surge in imports of clothing from China gave a foretaste of the scale of the challenges to be expected to follow from the size of the Chinese economy and the speed of its growth, with similar impact from India likely to follow; and Chinese accession to the WTO in 2001 was to make it harder for the Union to react with anti-dumping measures. While progress was nevertheless made with the Doha Round, the EU and the US still found it hard to negotiate reductions in their agricultural protection that would induce the G20 to respond positively enough. Whatever the outcome, there will be consideration of the viability of further trade rounds that have to be approved unanimously by 150 states, and of whether a different route towards international trade liberalization will be required; and the Union will have to consider whether, and if so how, its own experience of the last half-century can be applied in the wider world.

The EU, its neighbourhood, and the developing world

Whereas relations with the US are important for all member states, individual states have special relationships with particular countries in most of the rest of the world; and many of these became shared by the Union as a whole.

This, like much else, stems from the Treaty of Rome. France wanted advantages for its colonies, and made this a condition for ratification of the treaty. So the Community as a whole granted free entry to imports from them and provided aid through the European Development Fund (EDF). The same applied to territories relating to Belgium, Italy, and the Netherlands; and the resulting association was the original basis for the present Cotonou Convention. French pressure also led to preferential agreements for Morocco and Tunisia; and these were the forerunners of the present far-reaching system of agreements with neighbouring states.

After they became independent, the association with former colonies was transmuted through a Convention that provided for joint institutions: a Council of Ministers, Committee of Ambassadors, and Assembly of Parliamentarians. Following British accession, the Commonwealth countries of Africa, the Caribbean, and the Pacific joined in negotiating the Lomé Convention. This broadened the participation to include most of Africa and the Caribbean islands, as well as a number of islands in the Pacific, known collectively as the ACP countries. It removed some vestiges of the colonial system and has expanded the aid towards a level of €3 billion a year since the 1990s, together with money to cushion the associates against falls in their income from commodity exports.

The Lomé Convention was renewed for the fifth time at Cotonou in the year 2000, in difficult circumstances. For the associates were disturbed by the erosion of the margins of preference as tariffs had been reduced in successive Gatt rounds; and the Union was concerned that, despite the massive quantities of aid, almost all of Africa remained in bad shape, owing at least partly to poor governance. Enough was at stake, however, to win the agreement to the fifth Convention, both of the EU's partners, with the renewal of the aid programme, and of its member states, with the Convention's recognition that adequate performance

Direction of EU trade in goods by region, 2004

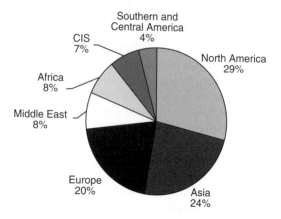

Exports

Southern and
Central America
4%

CIS
7%

Africa
8%

Middle East
8%

Europe
20%

North America
29%

Asia
24%

Total exports: €1158.7 billion

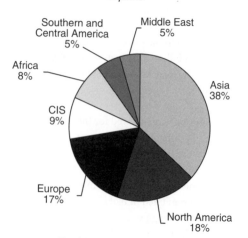

Imports

Southern and
Central America
5%

Middle East
5%

Africa
8%

CIS
9%

Europe
17%

Asia
38%

North America
18%

Total imports: €1231.3 billion

EU's partners in the Lomé Convention

The Lomé Convention links the EU to 79 African, Caribbean, and Pacific (ACP) states, giving them free and preferential entry for their exports to the EU and aid for their economic and social development:

Angola	Dominica	Mali
Antigua and Barbuda	Dominican Republic	Marshall Islands
Bahamas	Eritrea	Mauritania
Barbados	Ethiopia	Mauritius
Belize	Fiji	Micronesia
Benin	Gabon	Mozambique
Botswana	Gambia, The	Namibia
Burkina Faso	Ghana	Nauru
Burundi	Grenada	Niger
Cabo Verde	Equatorial Guinea	Nigeria
Cameroun	Guinea-Bissau	Niue
Central African Republic	Guyana	Palau
Chad	Haiti	Papua New Guinea
Comores	Jamaica	Rwanda
Congo	Kenya	São Tomé & Príncipe
Congo Democratic Republic	Kiribati	Samoa
Cook Islands	Lesotho	Sénégal
Côte D'Ivoire	Liberia	Seychelles
Cuba	Madagascar	Sierra Leone
Djibouti	Malawi	

Solomon Islands	Suriname	Tuvalu
Somalia	Swaziland	Uganda
South Africa	Tanzania	Vanuatu
St Kitts and Nevis	Timor-Lester	Zambia
St Lucia	Togo	Zimbabwe
St Vincent and The Grenadines	Tonga	
Sudan	Trinidad and Tobago	

in governance would be a criterion for the allocation of aid, and that the associates were to prepare their economies to join the Union in a free trade area in 20 years' time. Through the 1990s, moreover, the EU laid growing emphasis in its external relations on human rights, and the Lomé Convention requires the participants to respect them.

By the end of the 1970s the Community also had a network of agreements according preferences and assistance to states around the Mediterranean, with content not unlike that of the Lomé Convention but without the multilateral institutions. The network included all the North African states – save Libya which declined to participate – together with Israel, Lebanon, and, at one remove from the Mediterranean, Jordan and Syria.

By the 1990s, a combination of economic difficulties, political instability, and rapid population growth in most of these countries, with consequent pressure to migrate to Europe, caused growing anxiety in the Union, particularly among its southern states. The outcome was a conference of ministers from the Union and its Mediterranean partners, held in Barcelona in 1995, which launched a 'Euro-Mediterranean process' aimed at building a

Cotonou Convention, 2000–2020

The EU and ACP states (see Box 10.1) agreed in 2000 to renew the Lomé Convention for the fifth time, for a 20-year period. The resultant Cotonou Convention can be revised every five years and the aid protocols are also to be limited to five-year periods. The ACP-EU Council of Ministers meets yearly to review progress.

- *Trade* is at the heart of the agreement. Negotiations between the EU and each ACP state for 'economic partnership agreements' are to result by 2008 in a new trading arrangement intended to lead to an EU-ACP free trade area by 2020. Meanwhile the free or preferential entry to the EU is to be retained.

- *Aid* has been set at 13.5 billion euros for the first seven years, on top of 9.5 billion euros already allocated but not yet spent. Good performance in use of aid is to be rewarded.

- *Poverty reduction* is to be a favoured focus for development strategies.

- *Non-state actors* are to be encouraged to participate in the development process.

- *Political dialogue* indicates a harder-nosed EU approach, with good governance, respect for human rights, democratic principles, and the rule of law as criteria for aid policy, and with action against corruption.

Cotonou is coloured by the EU's disappointment with the results of the preceding Lomé I-IV, attributed to poor governance in many countries. Given this starting point, the development of an EU-ACP free trade area is a very ambitious idea.

EU member states

Other member of European Economic
Area (Iceland, Liechtenstein, Norway)

EU candidate countries
(Croatia, Macedonia, Turkey)

EU potential countries (Albania, Bosnia &
Herzegovina, Montenegro, Serbia)

European Neighbourhood Policy members
(Algeria, America, Azerbaijan, Belarus,
Egypt Georgia, Isreal, Jordan, Lebanon,
Libya, Moldova, Morocco, Palestinian
Authority, Syria, Tunisia, Ukraine)

Map 4 The EU's neighbourhood

wide range of multilateral links across the basin. However, the headline goal of the process – a free trade area by 2005 – was soon to founder on the political differences of the partners and the constant distraction of the Eastern enlargement.

With the coming of that enlargement, the Union engaged in a wholesale review of its links with its neighbours, with a particular eye on trying to keep the Union an open and accessible grouping. Thus it was in 2003 that the Commission proposed replacing the Euro-Mediterranean process, PHARE, and TACIS with a European Neighbourhood Policy. In 2007, these former programmes were formally incorporated into the ENP, supported by a new financial instrument that will provide some €1.7 billion a year for cross-border cooperation, the development of civil society, and technical assistance.

While the ENP represents a significant commitment on the part of the EU to these countries, it remains to be seen whether it will have any significant impact on the development of a more stable, democratic, or prosperous environment around the EU's borders.

Asia, Latin America, and generalized preferences

Britain, on joining the Community, managed to secure satisfactory terms for Commonwealth countries from Africa, the Caribbean, and the Pacific. But no special arrangement was agreed for the Asian members of the Commonwealth – India, Pakistan (which then included Bangladesh), Sri Lanka, Malaysia, Hong Kong, and Singapore – most of whose exports had entered Britain tariff-free under Commonwealth preference. The damage was limited, however, because in 1971 the Community was among the first to adopt a Generalized System of Preferences (GSP), according preferential entry to imports from almost all Third World countries that did not already benefit from the Lomé Convention or the Mediterranean agreements; and this reduced the discrimination against most Asian and Latin American

Shares of official development aid from EU, US, Japan, and others, 2005

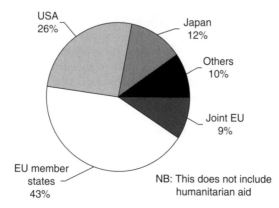

USA
26%

Japan
12%

Others
10%

Joint EU
9%

EU member
states
43%

NB: This does not include
humanitarian aid

Development aid from EU and member states by destination, 2004

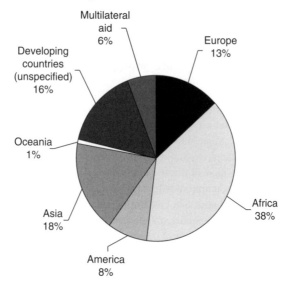

Multilateral
aid
6%

Europe
13%

Developing
countries
(unspecified)
16%

Oceania
1%

Asia
18%

America
8%

Africa
38%

countries. The system was less favourable than it may sound because for 'sensitive' (that is, the more competitive) products there were quotas limiting the preferences to quantities fixed in advance for each product and each member state. But the generalized preferences nevertheless helped to strengthen links with less-developed countries.

While the margins of preference that the GSP affords less-developed countries have declined along with the reduction of the general level of tariffs, their links with the EU through its aid programmes have become increasingly important. These amount to some €6 billion a year, including both humanitarian aid and the development aid for ACP countries and the ENP. The Community has also concluded bilateral trade and cooperation agreements to strengthen its links with major developing countries, including India, Mexico, and Brazil; it has agreements with regional groups such as ASEAN (the Association of South-East Asian Nations); and since Portugal and Spain joined the Community in 1986, their special links with Latin America have been added to those of other member states in Africa and Asia.

While the economic impact of the agreements, preferences, and aid can hardly be measured and may not have been very great, the Union has gained political credit which may be of help in the future development of its relationships with Asian, African, and Latin American countries.

Money

Whereas its common tariff had made the Community a trading power equivalent to the US, before the euro it had no monetary instrument that could become the equal of the dollar in the international monetary system. The challenge to American hegemony was one of the motives behind the long-standing French support for a single currency. The fluctuations of dollar exchange rates were uncomfortable for other member states too. The dollar's weakness first disrupted the attempt to create a single currency in the early 1970s, then spurred Europeans into taking the first major step of monetary integration with the establishment of the European Monetary System in 1979. In the 1980s the US policy of high interest rates, designed to counter inflation, provoked a debt crisis in many developing countries, restricting their development for up to a decade.

When those who manage a dominant currency have to choose between dealing with a domestic problem and taking account of the impact on other economies that are influenced by their choice, they naturally choose their domestic interests. Europeans experienced this in the 1990s when high German interest rates, designed to control inflation following German unification, exacerbated recession in other countries influenced by the dominant deutschmark; and this gave added edge to their support for the single currency, with a monetary policy tailored to the needs of the participants as a whole. While that remedy is not available to deal with the dollar's dominance in the world system, the euro can be the basis for a countervailing monetary power.

Thus the euro is another source of money with a different economic cycle, which can counteract the dollar's influence when it works against other countries' interests; and the wide swinging of the euro's exchange rate against the dollar during the past few years has been inconvenient for business on both sides. Despite the fact that the Union's monetary policies have initially been inward-looking, the euro could, however, become the basis for an exchange rate policy that favours international monetary stability. But it is handicapped by the weakness of its arrangements for conducting such a policy, with responsibility divided between the European Central Bank and the Council of finance ministers. The euro might, moreover, along with other major currencies, help to initiate an international system for stabilizing exchange rates. But here its institutional weakness is compounded by the veto that each minister retains over such decisions. The Union will be unable to act responsibly in the international monetary system without appropriate institutional reform. Nor is it likely to exert its due influence in the International Monetary Fund until a common policy is represented there with a single voice. So the Union has not yet made full use of the opportunity that the euro offers to replace American hegemony with a more equal relationship, such as the common commercial policy has long since done with respect to trade.

Security: peacekeeping and climate change

American hegemony in defence will, however, remain unchallenged for as long ahead as can be contemplated. Not only would Europeans have to undertake vast expenditure in any attempt to become independent of American strategic power, but the force thus acquired would also have to be controlled by a solidly established democratic European state with a number of years of reliable decision-taking behind it. So Europeans continue to depend on Nato's American-led strategic shield; and their efforts in the field of defence will be mainly to contribute to peacekeeping and peacemaking, particularly in actions sponsored by the United Nations. For defence of the Union's territory against major threats, Europeans will continue to depend on American protection.

It would be unwise to assume that such protection would never be needed, in what is becoming a multipolar world in strategic as well as economic terms, and where a growing number of states have weapons of mass destruction. Military threats to the Union's interests could, moreover, emerge with which the Americans may be unable or unwilling to deal. So the Union is likely to continue building its defence capacity as well as to keep the alliance in repair, while at the same time using its soft power to further the development of a safer world.

The Union did, as we saw in Chapter 8, resume the development of its military activities without much delay, following the internal divisions during the build-up to the American intervention in Iraq. Before the end of 2003, the European Council unanimously approved Javier Solana's proposal for an EU strategy to strengthen security around the Union and in the international order. In 2004, the Nato force in Bosnia was replaced by the EU force of 7,000 troops, with Nato assets and capabilities; and smaller but significant operations were undertaken in Georgia, Macedonia, and the Democratic Republic of Congo – the latter a precursor of the project for establishing battle groups which was launched in the same year. By 2006, the Union sent a peacekeeping force of some 8,000 troops to Lebanon after the war there between Hizbollah and Israel.

Thus the Union continued creating a significant capacity for military contributions to peacekeeping and peacemaking, a most important complement to which is its capacity to contribute to the civilian elements of peacekeeping, together with its experience in assisting the building of democratic states. One example, which can follow directly from a successful military mission, is the police missions, such as the Union has provided in Bosnia, where in 2003 it took over from a UN Police Task Force, followed by others in Macedonia, Democratic Republic of Congo, and Palestinian Territories. More broadly, it has much experience of assisting with the development of political, judicial, and administrative institutions, and the structures of civil society, particularly among Central and East European states preparing themselves for accession, as well as in the West Balkans and farther afield; and this has great potential importance for wider application in a world in which failed or failing states can be a serious security risk, while solidly based democracies can contribute much to stable international relations.

The common foreign policy element of the CFSP has been developed alongside the ESDP, ably assisted by Javier Solana representing the Union in, for example, the quartet of UN, US, Russia, and EU working on the road map for the two-state resolution of the Israel-Palestine problem, and, along with the representatives of France, Germany, and the UK, in the sensitive talks with Iran about uranium enrichment. This, with the economic implications in both cases, strongly suggests the merit of the provision in the mandate for the Reform Treaty for combining the functions of the High Representative with those of a Vice-President of the Commission, with influence over the Commission's external policies.

The environment is also a vital aspect of security, with climate change among the gravest threats to the welfare, and perhaps the lives, of the world's people; and the Union has made the major contribution to international efforts to deal with it. In 1986, when it had become evident that chlorofluorocarbons (CFCs) could destroy the ozone layer and thus endanger life on Earth, the EC succeeded in breaking a deadlock in negotiations for the Montreal Protocol to the UN Framework Convention on Climate Change, thus halting the degradation. Then in 1997 the Union played the leading part in the negotiations for the UNFCCC's Kyoto Protocol to stem the emissions of carbon dioxide and other greenhouse gases, which are generating a potentially disastrous degree of global warming. Despite intractable American resistance to targets as well as to the assistance required by developing countries for the necessary technological transformation, the EU ensured that there was agreement on the target of cutting emission by 8% below 1990 emissions by 2012. It also secured sufficient ratifications, in the teeth of energetic American opposition, for the Protocol to enter into force in February 2005; and the final ratification required was that of Russia, which appears to have been encouraged by the Union's use of an instrument of its common commercial policy, as the EU almost simultaneously reciprocated with its formal acceptance of Russia's coveted entry into the WTO.

Having concluded that global emissions need to be cut by 60% by mid-century and adopted that target for its own emissions, the EU has a compelling interest in securing similar commitments from as many states as possible; and it will do what it can, in negotiations for the commitment period of the Kyoto Protocol that is to start in 2113, to lead the other states in that direction.

The Union's role in the world

Too much American hegemony is dangerous for Americans as well as for others. Overwhelming power can lead to rash

17. **President of the European Commission, José Manuel Barroso, with Romano Prodi, George W. Bush, and Shinzo Abe at the 2007 G8 summit in Heiligendamm**

decisions; and the burden is too great for one country to carry alone. China seems likely to catch up with the US during the first half of this century as a military as well as economic power, with unpredictable consequences; and India may well follow. But the EU has the potential to be, much sooner, at least an equal partner with the US with respect to the economy, the environment, and soft security, though not defence.

Indeed, the EU's long-standing parity with the US in the world trading system has shown what can be done when sufficiently effective institutions dispose of a common instrument. The euro offers a basis for a similar performance in the international monetary system, if the institutions for external monetary policy are adequately reformed. For action on global climate change the Union should be able, again with some strengthening of its institutions, to maintain its leading role. Soft security, including the civilian aspects of keeping the peace, is a field in which it is developing a capacity that could become an essential counterpart for American military power; and the military instruments that the EU is creating also open up opportunities to perform a complementary role.

Adjustment to such changes in power relationships is always hard for those who have been on top. But it should not be too hard for Americans to adjust to a more powerful European Union, with a society that shares so much in so many ways; with four decades of reasonable cooperation in the field of trade where both already have equivalent strength; and with no prospect of rivalry in the field of military power. Having adjusted to an equal partnership with the EU in most other fields, it should be easier for the US to adjust to changes in relationships with other emergent powers, particularly as the EU will be well placed, with its network of relations with countries around the world, to advance the process of creating a stable world system that accommodates them.

The Union's own experience of institutions, policies, and attitudes that have helped the member states to live together in peace for half a century, together with its worldwide network of relationships, should indeed enable it to influence others to move in a similar direction. But Monnet's idea that such institutions might serve to create a prosperous and peaceful world could be realized only under quite exacting conditions. The necessary sharing of sovereignty is possible only among pluralist democracies that are willing to accept a common rule of law, and have the capacity to develop common legislative institutions to enact it and a system of government to implement policies within it. These conditions apply to a large extent within the Union, but in many parts of the world they do not. Meanwhile the Union can assist efforts to develop such conditions where they do not yet exist and to undertake Community-type developments where they do; and it can support steps to help the United Nations and other international organizations to become more effective, while recognizing that institutions of a community type cannot be created at that level until pluralist democracy becomes the norm throughout the world. But Union policies which point towards such an outcome are in the long-term interest of its states and citizens; and even if a very long time-scale has to be envisaged, the European experience has shown that initiating a process which leads in that direction can already begin to transform relations between states.

Chapter 11
Much accomplished ... but what next?

The European Union has come a long way since the process of its construction was launched by the Schuman declaration in 1950. War has indeed become unthinkable among the member states, which now include most European countries. The preceding chapters have shown how institutions, powers, and policies have been put in place to deal with matters beyond the reach of governments of the individual states. But they have also shown that the Union needs further reform if it is to promote the interests of its people adequately in an increasingly problematic world. Now we can try to sum up what has been done and venture some thoughts about the future.

Do the powers and instruments match the aims?

The Union has been able to achieve its aims where it has the powers and instruments as well as the institutions with which to act. The powers and instruments can be legislative, such as the framework for the single market; fiscal, as with the budget or the common external tariff; or financial, as with the aid programmes, the European Investment Bank, and most importantly the single currency. Cooperation based on the powers and instruments of member states can be useful, but would not achieve much without the hard core of common powers and instruments.

The single market legislation provides a framework for economic strength and prosperity, even if it remains incomplete in some significant sectors and will need further development to cater adequately for the new economy including e-commerce and information technology; and, for member states that have adopted the euro, the single currency completes the single market in the monetary domain.

The budget has transferred resources to sectors deemed to require support, originally to agriculture but increasingly to less-developed regions and member states. While the agricultural budget has generated conflict, the structural funds to assist development of poorer regions have been more generally favoured; and the enlargement to Central and Eastern Europe reinforces the case for larger funds.

Thus the Union has many of the necessary powers in the economic field. The same can be said of the environment, where the most pressing need is to strengthen both internal and external action to limit the damage from climate change.

Social policy as embodied in the welfare state belongs largely, following the principle of subsidiarity, to the member states. That principle justifies Union involvement in some employment-related aspects of social policy, such as the prevention of social dumping by undercutting standards of health and safety at work. There is a grey area, including elements of social security and hours of work, where there is conflict between those who want to establish Union-wide standards and those who consider that differences rooted in differing social cultures should not be disturbed. Disagreements remain; but the latter view has gained ground.

While the economic and environmental aims and powers were promoted by interest groups as well as federalists, as was the free movement of workers across the internal frontiers, it was the federal idea that lay behind free movement for all within the Union, which has been accepted, apart from transitional derogations relating to new member states, by all save Denmark, Ireland, and the UK. But all participate in measures to combat cross-frontier crime.

In the field of its external relations, the Union's powers have been designed to defend and promote common interests, which include stability in the international economic and political system. The most potent instrument is the offer of accession, hence of participation in the Union's institutions and powers as a whole. But this is available only for European states; and other means have to be used to advance the Union's interests in the rest of the world.

The powers over external trade, together with the instrument of the common external tariff, have enabled the Union to serve its interest in liberal international trade as well as to turn what was American hegemony in this field into EU-US partnership. The protectionist common agricultural policy, working in the opposite direction, marred relations with many trading partners. Reforms to correct this distortion have taken far too long, but are being accomplished by stages. A combination of preferential arrangements and aid has strengthened links with most Third World countries.

Along with this influence in the world trading system, the Union has used its environmental powers to play the leading part in international negotiations to protect the ozone layer and limit the damage from climate change.

With the euro the Union has a potentially powerful instrument to wield in the international monetary system. But until it has adequate institutional arrangements for external monetary policy, its potential, which could convert American hegemony into partnership in this field too, is not likely to be realized.

For defence, American military dominance remains a fact which the EU's incremental approach to military integration is not designed to challenge, though it serves increasingly useful purposes. It is in the civil domain that the Union can complement American power, with civilian aspects of peacekeeping and, much more substantially, through its contribution to European and world stability in the economic, environmental, and political fields. The Union is uniquely placed to ease the transition from global American hegemony to a multipolar world, in which Euro-American partnership can play an essential part. The Union needs some new powers to accomplish this, together with further reform of the institutions to enable it to use the powers to good effect.

The institutions: how effective? how democratic?

Eurosceptics tend to regard 'closer integration' as undesirable without distinguishing between transfer of powers to the Union and reform of its institutions. But these are two very different questions. The transfer of powers is justified only where the Union can serve the citizens in ways that individual member states cannot; and the Union already has many of the powers indicated by the subsidiarity principle except in the field of defence. Once powers have been transferred, however, they will not serve the citizens' interests well enough unless they are wielded by effective and democratic Union institutions.

The political institutions require a context of the rule of law, which is ensured by the Court of Justice in matters of Community competence; and this has brought fundamental change in the relations among member states.

The Council, however, is not effective enough where the unanimity rule prevails, as was demonstrated by the inadequacy of single market legislation before qualified majority voting was applied. It has become more effective now that QMV applies to the majority of legislative acts as well as the whole of the budget;

but the Nice Treaty went only a modest part of the way towards the further extension that was needed. Unanimity and enhanced cooperation remain the practical procedures where the Union depends on the use of member states' instruments, as in the field of defence. But in line with the growth in the number of member states, there must be increasing doubts about the Union's capacity to act where unanimity still applies, for example with treaties of association and accession, nominations to some major posts in the institutions, and international agreements on exchange rate arrangements.

The Commission has substantial powers to fulfil its functions as the Community's executive, though its role in ensuring that member states do in fact carry out the administration that is delegated to them by the Community is not strong enough, and too much intervention by the Council and its network of committees in the execution of Community decisions hampers the Commission's effectiveness. The Commission's own administrative culture had also become a serious weakness, but the reforms effected after the European Parliament secured the Commission's resignation in March 1999 brought substantial improvement.

The part the Parliament then played in ensuring the Commission's resignation showed how democratic control can contribute to effectiveness. But the Parliament's impact on legislation and on the budget remains limited by the treaty, which is still far from putting it on a par with the Council for either. The Council has retained dominant power over the agricultural budget, though the Reform Treaty would convert this to co-decision; and the Parliament has performed creditably on the rest of the budget, and the legislative acts that it co-decides on level terms with the Council.

The Nice Treaty did little to increase the scope for co-decision; and this was a very serious omission. For in so far as it remains incomplete, the Union will be neglecting an essential means of securing citizens' support. Citizens are likely to become a centrifugal force unless they develop a commitment to the Union alongside that to their states; and it would be unwise to ignore the track record of representative democracy as a major element in citizenship. So long as citizens do not see the Parliament as an equal of the Council, they are not likely to regard it as a sufficiently important channel of representation. The Council, representing the states, is an essential part of the Union's legislature too. But despite the progress in holding legislative sessions in public, it remains at the centre of an opaque system of quasi-diplomatic negotiation. Representation in a powerful house of the citizens may well be a condition of their support for the Union over the longer term.

The success of the provision for gender equality at work shows how citizens' rights can also generate support for the Union. The treaty provides for a number of other rights, mostly connected with work, as well as requiring the institutions to respect the European Convention of Human Rights. The Charter of Fundamental Rights that was drafted by a convention of MEPs, MPs, and government representatives, and welcomed by the European Council at Nice, will be of help to citizens, though the extent to which it becomes legally binding depends on the enactment of the Reform Treaty. But most important of all for the citizens will be the Union's general effectiveness in doing things that are necessary for them. It must be seen to be doing such things at a time when it confronts major challenges, both internally and in the world at large; and it is more likely to do so if the Reform Treaty, strengthening the institutions with more QMV and co-decision, together with the more powerful High Representative, enters into force.

Flexible versus federal

The word 'flexible' is used approvingly in much British discourse on Europe to denote both the avoidance of excessive regulation in the economy and, politically, an aversion to proposals, apart from completion of the single market, for common instruments and legally binding commitments such as have characterized the European Community pillar of the Union.

Flexibility in the economic sense has been successful in the development of the swiftly changing contemporary economy; and this has been increasingly recognized in the EU. But flexibility in the political sense is not appropriate for matters which the individual states are unable to handle effectively. One recent example was the avoidance of sufficient common instruments and binding commitments to provide a reliable core for the programme of the Lisbon Agenda, around which the cooperation through the open method of coordination would have had more chance of success. Another was the refusal of the existing member states to increase the size of the Union's budget for structural funds, or reduce their own benefits from them, in order to give enough support for developing the capacity of the Central and East Europeans for making their full contribution to the success of the Union as a whole, as the cohesion policy for Greece, Ireland, Portugal, and Spain had done.

A vital challenge for the longer term is also to ensure that European enterprises will be among the leaders in technological development; and in some sectors such as aircraft and satellites, this requires large and long-term investments of public money. But the progress of Airbus has been interrupted by intergovernmental wrangling, and sufficient Union support for the Galileo satellite project remains in doubt. A common European effort is needed to support such projects, which are too large for single European governments; and in so far as some member states are not ready to participate, there can be structured enhanced cooperation among those that are.

Other instances of enhanced cooperation may arise as a result of problems for some participants in the eurozone which, despite its success in many respects, has led to reduced employment and growth for those with less economic flexibility or control over inflationary pressures in their economies. While reforms making for greater economic flexibility are particularly important, given the disciplines of the eurozone, further measures of enhanced cooperation may be required, such as a loan facility and measures to foster economic regeneration in zones facing particular difficulties; and this could provide additional momentum for a core group of states, such as the eurozone, resolved to go beyond what the reluctant British and some others are prepared to do.

A harbinger was the speech made by Joschka Fischer, 'in his personal capacity' though he was then German Foreign Minister, in which he proposed that a vanguard group should push ahead with political integration within the Union as a step towards eventual federation including all member states. This evoked significant support and was one source of the demand for the Nice Treaty's Protocol that led to the convening of the Convention which drafted the Constitutional Treaty, signed by all the then 25 member states though rejected by the French and Dutch referendums; and the IGC on the Reform Treaty indicates that there are likely to be specific measures of further political integration, through enhanced cooperation, if resistance from the UK or others frustrates too many proposals for the Union's future development. In the field of its external development, however, the British could become more likely than in the past to support adequate strengthening of the Union's powers and institutions.

A large part of the divergence between the approaches of the British and of most other member states has stemmed from the differing experiences in World War Two, which was more traumatic for most of the continental nations. So while much of the progress in building the Union has had economic motives, it was a profound desire to consolidate peace and security that underlay the major shifts towards the sharing of sovereignty, such as the European Coal and Steel Community, and the Treaties of Rome and Maastricht. The British accepted the merits of economic integration but resisted the sharing of sovereignty, accepting only what was required to participate in the large market or to avoid losing too much political influence.

But governments and large numbers of citizens throughout the Union, including the British, are conscious of the many and various sources of insecurity in the world, and share the desire for progress towards a safer world based on a more effective multilateral system. So they may also be able to accept the implication of such sharing of sovereignty as may be necessary in order to enhance sufficiently the Union's capacity for action towards that end. Its military capabilities for peacekeeping are growing; and while it is not likely to become a great military power, it can become the world's principal peacemaker across an impressive range of soft power. It can enhance its contribution to prosperity and stability in the global economy in the fields of trade, aid, and external monetary policy; it can help, as it has shown in the West Balkans and elsewhere, to build and sustain viable democratic states; and it has led the world in action to prevent ruinous climate change. It could moreover do much, as a very great civilian power, to ease the transition to a world in which the United States will be joined by China, then India, as very great powers in the military sense too; and it can help them and others to develop an increasingly effective United Nations. All this will be significantly enhanced if the Reform Treaty, approved by the IGC in October 2007, is ratified by member states.

There is a wide consensus among member states, not least the UK, about the validity of such aims. But there has not been agreement on how to apply the Union's full weight in achieving them. A major difficulty has been the reluctance of many, again not least the British, to accept the allocation of resources to the Union and to strengthen its institutions in ways that could make it sufficiently effective; and this implies the acceptance of an adequate core of legally binding commitments and common instruments, with institutional reform to make the Union properly effective and democratic. The word 'federal' is a convenient and accurate abbreviation for the words following 'core of' in the preceding sentence, whether or not such commitments, instruments, and reformed institutions lead eventually to a federation. The word is less important than what it represents. Its use, if properly defined, would, however, clarify thinking as well as facilitate communication with those who use it. A rose by any other name would smell as sweet. But it is better to give the rose a name consisting of one word rather than seventeen.

The British, as much as other Europeans, sense their exposure to the mounting sources of insecurity in the world today. So Britain should be able to play a fully constructive part in supporting reforms of the Union's existing powers and institutions that would enable it to realize its great potential influence towards creating a safer and more prosperous world.

References

References, in line with the nature of this series, have been kept to the minimum of quotations whose source is not obvious from the text.

Chapter 2

Spinelli called the Single Act a 'dead mouse' in his speech to the European Parliament on 16 January 1986, reprinted in Altiero Spinelli, *Discorsi al Parlamento Europeo*, ed. Pier Virgilio Dastoli (Bologna, 1987), p. 369. Jenkins recalled his choice of a theme to 'move Europe forward' in *European Diary 1977–1981* (London, 1989), pp. 22–3.

Chapter 3

Margaret Thatcher spoke of 'a European super-state' in her *Britain and Europe: Text of the Speech Delivered in Bruges by the Prime Minister on 20th September 1988* (London: Conservative Political Centre, 1988), p. 4.

Chapter 7

Bevin and Victoria Station is to be found in Michael Charlton, *The Price of Victory* (London, 1983), pp. 43–4.

Chapter 9

Poos on 'the hour of Europe' was reported in the *New York Times*,
29 June 1991, p. 4.

Chapter 10

The Community 'as an example' is from Jean Monnet, *Les États-Unis
d'Europe ont commencé: Discours et allocutions 1952–1954*
(Paris, 1955), p. 128.
The EC as 'the most important member of Gatt' is from Lawrence
B. Krause, *European Economic Integration and the United States*
(Washington, DC, 1968), p. 225.
The EC and 'effective international law-making' is from Tommaso
Padoa-Schioppa, *Financial and Monetary Integration in Europe:
1990, 1992 and Beyond* (London and New York, 1990), p. 28.

Further reading

There is a great deal of academic literature on the European Union, but not so many reliable books for the general reader or for those who are just setting out to acquire academic knowledge.

Of the many texts that provide **general introductions**, John Pinder's *The Building of the European Union* (Oxford, 3rd edn, 1998, 297 pp.), while more detailed than the present volume, is fairly accessible. A more ample academic introduction can be found in Desmond Dinan's *Ever-Closer Union* (Basingstoke, 3rd edn, 2005, 664 pp.). A federalist view of the way in which the EU has developed is to be found in Michael Burgess, *Federalism and European Union: The Building of Europe, 1950–2000* (London, 2000, 290 pp.). Chapters on all the main policies are to be found in Helen Wallace, William Wallace, and Mark Pollack (eds), *Policy-Making in the European Union* (Oxford, 5th edn, 2005, 570 pp.). A wide range of subjects is also covered in the *Annual Review* of the *Journal of Common Market Studies* (Oxford).

Timothy Bainbridge and Anthony Teasdale, *The Penguin Companion to the European Union* (Harmondsworth, 3rd edn, 2004, 592 pp.) is an accurate and convenient **work of reference**.

For those who appreciate a **biographical** approach to the subject, the history of the EC up to the 1970s is seen through the eyes of its principal founding father in Jean Monnet's *Memoirs* (London, 1978, 544 pp.). Flavour and substance of the Delors period, from 1985 to 1994, are to be found in Charles Grant, *Inside the House that Jacques Built* (London, 1994, 305 pp.); and the political ideas and strategy of Delors are analysed in detail by George Ross in his *Jacques Delors and European Integration* (Cambridge, 1995). A range of leading actors in the uniting of Europe are given lively treatment in Martyn Bond, Julie Smith, and William Wallace (eds), *Eminent Europeans* (London, 1996, 321 pp.). Hugo Young provides unsurpassed insights into the development of British relations with the EU, through chapters on a dozen British protagonists and antagonists from Churchill to Blair, in *This Blessed Plot* (Basingstoke, 1998, 558 pp.).

There is not much that is easy to read and gives a true and fair view of how the **institutions** work. Neil Nugent's *The Government and Politics of the European Union* (Basingstoke, 6th edn, 2006, 630 pp.) is reliable and comprehensive, but not light reading. Michelle Cini's *European Union Politics* (Oxford, 2nd edn, 2007, 496 pp.) opens up a wide range of subjects to the reader. Shorter explanations of the institutions can be found in the chapter on 'Institutions or Constitution' in *The Building of the European Union* and in Helen Wallace's chapter on 'An Institutional Anatomy and Five Policy Modes' in Wallace, Wallace, and Pollack (eds), *Policy-Making in the European Union* (both books cited above). Chapters 7–10 of Dinan's *Ever Closer Union* (also cited above) deal with main institutions. Julie Smith's *Europe's Elected Parliament* (Sheffield, 1999, 198 pp.) is readable and informative. The literature on the Court of Justice and the Court of First Instance is mainly by the lawyers for the lawyers, but pp. 289–307 of Dinan's book offer a good summary.

Ali El-Agraa's *The Euroean Union: Economics and Policies* (Cambridge, 8th edn, 2007, 592 pp.) has the most current overview of **economics and economic policies**. Lord Cockfield's *The European Union: Creating the Single Market* (Chichester, 1994, 185 pp.) is a lucid and entertaining account by the man who did most to create it, while Alasdair Young, in 'The Single Market' (chapter in Wallace, Wallace, and Pollack (eds) *Policy-Making in the European Union*) brings you up to date. The budget is well explained by Iain Begg and Nigel Grimwade in *Paying for Europe* (Sheffield, 1998, 200 pp.), and the CAP by C. Ritson and D. R. Harvey (eds) in *The Common Agricultural Policy* (Wallingford, Oxon, 2nd edn, 1997, 448 pp.). Regional policies are covered in David Allen, 'Cohesion and the Structural Funds' (chapter in Wallace, Wallace, and Pollack (eds) *Policy-Making in the European Union*).

Useful summaries of the EU's **environmental policies** are given annually in Nigel Haig (ed.), *Manual of Environmental Policy: The EU and Britain* (Oxford: Elsevier Science), and in the *Environment Guide* of The EU Committee of the American Chamber of Commerce in Brussels.

Most of the literature on the EU's **external relations** is about the Common Foreign and Security Policy, though the external economic policies remain more effective and important. Simon Nuttall provides an authoritative overview in *European Foreign Policy* (Oxford, 2000, 280 pp.) and a variety of approaches to the CFSP are to be found in Walter Carlsnaes, Helen Sjusen, and Brian White (eds), *Contemporary European Foreign Policy* (London, 2004, 288 pp.). While the full impact of the eastern enlargement is still being digested, Neil Nugent's *European Union Enlargement* (London, 2004, 328 pp.) and John O'Brennan's *The Eastern Enlargement of the European Union* (London, 2006, 239 pp.) provide helpful snapshots of the Union as it moves into a new phase.

The **Area of Freedom, Security and Justice** is also a fast-moving subject: Sandra Lavenex's and William Wallace's chapter on 'Justice and Home Affairs' in Wallace, Wallace, and Pollack (eds) *Policy-Making in the European Union* gives a good overview.

Across the board, the EU's website – http://europa.eu – is a vast quarry of information, from the very basic through to the highly technical.

Chronology 1946–2007

1940s

19 September 1946	Churchill calls for 'a kind of United States of Europe'.
5 June 1947	Marshall Plan announced.
16 April 1948	OEEC created to coordinate Marshall Plan for West European states.
4 April 1949	Signature of North Atlantic Treaty establishing Nato.
5 May 1949	Establishment of Council of Europe

1950s

9 May 1950	Schuman Declaration launches negotiations to establish ECSC, as 'a first step in the federation of Europe'.
18 April 1951	The Six (Belgium, France, Germany, Italy, Luxembourg, Netherlands) sign ECSC Treaty.
27 May 1952	The Six sign European Defence Community (EDC) Treaty.
27 July 1952	ECSC Treaty enters into force.
30 August 1954	French National Assembly shelves EDC Treaty.
20 October 1954	The Six and UK found WEU.
1–2 June 1955	Foreign ministers of the Six agree at Messina to launch negotiations resulting in EEC and Euratom.

25 March 1957	Rome Treaties establishing EEC and Euratom signed.
1 January 1958	Rome Treaties enter into force.

1960s

3 May 1960	Efta established by Austria, Denmark, Norway, Portugal, Sweden, Switzerland, UK.
14 December 1960	OEEC becomes OECD, including Canada and US as well as West European states.
31 July, 10 August 1961	Ireland, Denmark, UK apply to join Communities. Norway applies in April 1962.
14 January 1962	Common agricultural policy agreed by the Six.
14 January 1963	President de Gaulle terminates accession negotiations.
1 July 1965	France breaks off negotiations on financing CAP, boycotts Council until January 1966.
28–9 January 1966	Luxembourg 'Compromise' agreed. France returns to Council insisting on unanimity when 'very important' interests at stake.
11 May 1967	UK reactivates membership application, followed by Ireland, Denmark, Norway. De Gaulle still demurs.
1 July 1968	Customs union completed 18 months ahead of schedule.
1–2 December 1969	Hague Summit agrees arrangements for financing CAP, and resumption of accession negotiations.

1970s

22 April 1970	Amending Treaty signed, giving Community all revenue from common external tariff and agricultural import levies plus share of value-added tax, and European Parliament some powers over budget.
27 October 1970	Council establishes 'EPC' procedures for foreign policy cooperation.

22 March 1971	Council adopts plan to achieve Emu by 1980, soon derailed by international monetary turbulence.
22 January 1972	Accession Treaties of Denmark, Ireland, Norway, UK signed (but Norwegians reject theirs in referendum).
1 January 1973	Denmark, Ireland, UK join Community.
9–10 December 1974	Paris Summit decides to hold meetings three times a year as European Council and gives go-ahead for direct elections to European Parliament.
28 February 1975	Community and 46 African, Caribbean, and Pacific countries sign Lomé Convention.
18 March 1975	European Regional Development Fund established.
22 July 1975	Amending Treaty signed, giving European Parliament more budgetary powers and setting up Court of Auditors.
1–2 December 1975	European Council takes formal decision for direct elections.
7–8 April 1978	European Council endorses Joint Declaration of Parliament, Council, Commission, on fundamental rights.
4–5 December 1978	European Council establishes European Monetary System with Exchange Rate Mechanism based on ecu.
7, 10 June 1979	First direct elections to European Parliament.

1980s

1 January 1981	Greece becomes tenth member of Community.
14 February 1984	Draft Treaty on European Union, inspired by Spinelli, passed by big majority in European Parliament.
14, 17 June 1984	Second elections to European Parliament.
25–6 June 1984	Fontainebleau European Council agrees on rebate to reduce UK's net contribution to Community budget.

7 January 1985	New Commission takes office, Delors President.
14 June 1985	Schengen Agreement eliminating border controls signed by Belgium, France, Germany, Luxembourg, Netherlands.
28-9 June 1985	European Council approves Commission project to complete single market by 1992; considers proposals from Parliament's Draft Treaty; initiates IGC for Treaty amendment.
1 January 1986	Spain, Portugal accede, membership now 12.
17, 28 February 1986	Single European Act signed.
1 July 1987	Single European Act enters into force.
1 July 1988	Interinstitutional Agreement between Parliament, Council, Commission on budgetary discipline and procedure enters into force.
24 October 1988	Court of First Instance established.
15, 18 June 1989	Third elections to European Parliament.
9 November 1989	Fall of Berlin Wall. German Democratic Republic opens borders.
8-9 December 1989	European Council initiates IGC on Emu; all save UK adopt charter of workers' social rights.
1990s	
28 April 1990	European Council agrees policy on German unification and relations with Central and East European states.
29 May 1990	Agreement signed to establish European Bank for Reconstruction and Development.
19 June 1990	Second Schengen Agreement signed.
20 June 1990	EEC and Efta start negotiations to create European Economic Area (EEA).
25-6 June 1990	European Council decides to call IGC on political union, parallel with that on Emu.
3 October 1990	Unification of Germany and de facto enlargement of Community.
14-15 December 1990	European Council launches IGCs on Emu and political union.

9–10 December 1991	European Council agrees TEU (Maastricht Treaty).
16 December 1991	'Europe Agreements' with Poland, Hungary, Czechoslovakia signed; those with Czech Republic and Slovakia (successors to Czechoslovakia), Bulgaria, Estonia, Latvia, Lithuania, Romania, Slovenia follow at intervals.
7 February 1992	Maastricht Treaty signed.
2 May 1992	Agreement on EEA signed.
2 June 1992	Danish referendum rejects Maastricht Treaty.
14 September 1992	First ministerial meeting of participants in TACIS programme of assistance for CIS states.
20 September 1992	French referendum narrowly approves Maastricht Treaty.
6 December 1992	Swiss referendum rejects joining EEA; attempt to join EU shelved.
11–12 December 1992	European Council offers Denmark special arrangements to facilitate Treaty ratification; endorses Delors package of budgetary proposals; agrees to start accession negotiations with Austria, Norway, Sweden, Finland.
31 December 1992	Bulk of single market legislation completed on time.
18 May 1993	Second Danish referendum accepts Maastricht Treaty.
21–2 June 1993	Copenhagen European Council declares associated Central and East European states can join when they fulfil the political and economic conditions.
1 November 1993	Maastricht Treaty enters into force.
5 December 1993	Commission adopts White Paper on growth, competitiveness, employment.
9, 12 June 1994	Fourth elections to European Parliament.
15 July 1994	European Council nominates Santer to succeed Delors as Commission President.

28 November 1994	Norwegian referendum rejects accession.
1 January 1995	Austria, Finland, Sweden join, membership now 15.
12 July 1995	European Parliament appoints first Union Ombudsman.
26 July 1995	Member states sign Europol Convention.
27–8 November 1995	Euro-Mediterranean Conference in Barcelona.
31 December 1995	EC–Turkey customs union enters into force.
29 March 1996	IGC to revise Maastricht Treaty begins.
16 July 1997	Commission presents 'Opinions' on applications of ten Central and East European countries, and 'Agenda 2000' proposals to adapt EU policies for enlargement.
2 October 1997	Amsterdam Treaty signed.
12 March 1998	Accession negotiations open with Cyprus, Czech Republic, Estonia, Hungary, Poland, Slovenia.
3 May 1998	Council decides 11 states ready to adopt euro on 1 January 1999.
1 June 1998	European Central Bank established.
24–5 October 1998	European Council agrees measures of defence cooperation.
31 December 1998	Council fixes irrevocable conversion rates between euro and currencies of participating states.
1 January 1999	Euro becomes official currency of Austria, Belgium, Finland, France, Germany, Ireland, Italy, Luxembourg, Netherlands, Portugal, Spain.
15 March 1999	Commission resigns following report by independent committee on allegations of mismanagement and fraud.
24 March 1999	Prodi nominated new Commission President.
24–5 March 1999	European Council agrees on Agenda 2000.
1 May 1999	Amsterdam Treaty enters into force.
10–13 June 1999	Fifth elections to European Parliament.

10–11 December 1999	European Council decides on accession negotiations with six more states; recognizes Turkey as applicant; initiates IGC for Treaty revision.

2000

15 January 2000	Accession negotiations open with Bulgaria, Latvia, Lithuania, Malta, Romania, Slovakia.
20 June 2000	Lisbon European Council agrees measures for flexibility in EU economy.
23 June 2000	Lomé Convention V signed.
28 September 2000	Danish voters reject membership of euro in referendum.
7–10 December 2000	European Council concludes negotiations for Nice Treaty and welcomes Charter of Fundamental Rights.
1 January 2001	Greece becomes 12th member of the euro zone.
7 June 2001	Irish voters reject Treaty of Nice in a referendum.
14–15 December 2001	Laeken European Council agrees declaration on future of Union, opening way for a wholesale reform process.

2002

1 January 2002	Euro notes and coins enter into circulation.
28 February 2002	Convention on the Future of the EU opens in Brussels.
19 October 2002	Irish voters approve Treaty of Nice in a second referendum.
12–13 December 2002	Copenhagen European Council concludes accession negotiations with ten countries in Central and Eastern Europe and the Mediterranean.

2003

1 February 2003	Treaty of Nice enters into force.
14 September 2003	Swedish voters reject membership of euro in a referendum.

| 4 October 2003 | IGC opens to consider treaty reform on basis of Convention's draft EU constitution. |

2004

1 May 2004	Cyprus, Czech Republic, Estonia, Hungary, Latvia, Lithuania, Malta, Poland, Slovak Republic, and Slovenia join the Union, making 25 member states.
29 June 2004	Barroso nominated new Commission President.
29 October 2004	Heads of State and Government and the EU Foreign Ministers sign the Treaty establishing a Constitution for Europe.

2005

| 29 May, 1 June 2005 | French and Dutch voters reject Constitutional Treaty in referendums. |
| 3 October 2005 | Accession negotiations open with Turkey and Croatia. |

2007

1 January 2007	Bulgaria and Romania become the 26th and 27th member states of the Union. Slovenia becomes the 13th participant in eurozone.
23 March 2007	Berlin Declaration celebrating 50 years since the signing of the Treaties of Rome.
21–22 June 2007	Brussels European Council agrees to open IGC on Reform Treaty.

Glossary

Words in *italics* refer to other entries.

Accession: The process of joining the *European Union*. After accession treaties have been negotiated, all member states must ratify them and the European Parliament must give its assent.

Acquis Communautaire: The full set of the *European Union*'s legislative, regulatory, judicial, and normative output.

Agenda 2000: Measures to reform *common agricultural* and *cohesion policies* with a view to enlargement to Central and Eastern Europe.

Amsterdam Treaty: See *Treaty of Amsterdam*.

Area of Freedom, Security and Justice (**AFSJ**): The *Amsterdam Treaty* incorporated the *Schengen Agreements* in the *European Community*, providing for abolition of frontier controls; free movement of people; judicial and police cooperation against cross-border crime. Ireland, the UK, and to some extent Denmark opted out of the abolition of frontier controls and of the aspects involving EC institutions.

Asymmetric shocks: Affect different regions within an economy in different ways: a potential problem for the eurozone.

Barriers to trade: Tariffs and quotas have been eliminated from trade among member states. The aim of the single market, to eliminate the non-tariff barriers, has been largely achieved, though some still remain.

Budget of the *European Union*: Revenue comes from *own resources*; two-thirds of spending is on the *common agricultural* and *cohesion* policies.

Citizenship: The *Treaty on European Union* created a European citizenship, alongside member states' citizenships. Citizens are entitled to rights conferred by the treaties.

Cohesion policy: The *European Union*'s regional development policy, implemented through *structural funds* accounting for one-third of European Union *budget* spending.

Comitology: System of committees of member states' officials supervising the *Commission's* work on behalf of the *Council*.

Commission, European Commission: The main executive body of the *European Union*, comprising 27 Commissioners, responsible for different policy areas. In addition to its executive functions, the Commission initiates legislation and supervises compliance. The term 'Commission' is often used collectively for the Commission and its staff of some 23,000.

Committee of Permanent Representatives (Coreper): See *Council*.

Committee of the Regions: Comprises representatives of regional and local authorities. Provides opinions on legislation and issues reports on its own initiative.

Common agricultural policy (CAP): Much reformed, it still accounts for almost half of the *EU*'s budget spending, through its direct support of farmers and rural development.

Common Foreign and Security Policy (CFSP): Second *pillar* of the *European Union*, for intergovernmental cooperation on foreign policy and, using the capacities of *Western European Union*, defence. The

Secretary General of the *Council* is also the 'High Representative' who assists the Council *Presidency* in representing the European Union externally.

Community: See *European Community.*

Compulsory Expenditure (CE): Budgetary expenditure, largely for the *common agricultural policy*, over which the *Council* has more power than the *European Parliament*.

Constitutional Treaty: Signed in 2004, it provides for a recasting of the EU. The *pillars* would be abolished; posts of President of the *European Council* and Union Minister for Foreign Affairs created; the Charter of Fundamental Rights incorporated; co-decision and QMV extended; and the competences of the Union exhaustively listed for the first time. Its status is unclear following its rejection by referendums in 2005 in France and the Netherlands, despite ratification by the majority of member states.

Convention on the Future of Europe: Open forum of representatives of parliaments and governments set up in 2002 after the Laeken declaration by the *European Council* to discuss a complete redrawing of the EU. Under its chair, Valéry Giscard d'Estaing, it presented a Draft Treaty establishing a Constitution for Europe in 2003, which formed the basis of the *Constitutional Treaty*.

Cooperation in Justice and Home Affairs (CJHA): Former third *pillar* of the *European Union*, for cooperation relating to movement of people across frontiers and for combating cross-frontier crime. The *Treaty of Amsterdam* transferred much of the CJHA into the *Community's* new *Area of Freedom, Security and Justice*. Since Ireland and the UK opted out of AFSA, a reduced third pillar for *Police and Judicial Cooperation in Criminal Matters* remains.

Copenhagen Criteria: The benchmarks used by the EU for evaluating the suitability of states applying for membership. They cover: stable institutions guaranteeing democracy, the rule of law, human rights and respect for minorities; a functioning market economy; the ability to take on the *acquis* and support for the various aims of the European Union.

Council, Council of Ministers: Comprises representatives of member states at ministerial level. It amends and *votes* on legislation, supervises execution of *Community* policies, and is responsible for policies under the second and third *pillars*. It is supported by the Council Secretariat in Brussels, and by the Committee of Permanent Representatives and its system of committees (see *comitology*). The Council, with the *European Council*, is the *European Union's* most powerful political institution.

Court of First Instance: Judges cases in areas such as competition law and disputes between the institutions and their employees.

Court of Justice: The final judicial authority with respect to *Community* law. Its 27 judges, one from each member state sitting in Luxembourg, have developed an extensive case-law (see *European legal order*). The Court has ensured that the rule of law prevails in the Community.

Direct effect: See *European legal order*.

Directive: A *Community* legal act that is 'binding, as to the result to be achieved', but leaves to member states' authorities 'the choice of form and methods'.

Economic and Monetary Union (Emu): Thirteen member states participate in Emu, having satisfied the 'convergence criteria' of sound finance and irrevocably fixed their exchange rates with the euro, which replaced their currencies at the beginning of 2002. Monetary policy is the responsibility of the *European Central Bank* and the *European System of Central Banks*. There is a system for coordination of economic policy.

Economic and Social Committee (Ecosoc): Comprises representatives of employers, workers, and social groups. Provides opinions on *European Community* legislation and issues reports on its own initiative.

Electoral systems: In elections to the *European Parliament*, proportional representation is now used in all countries, since the UK adopted it for the 1999 elections.

Enhanced cooperation: Allows those states that want to integrate more closely than others in particular fields to do so within the *European Union* framework.

European Atomic Energy Community (Euratom): Established in 1957 alongside the *European Economic Community* to promote cooperation in the field of atomic energy; undertakes research and development for civilian purposes.

European Central Bank (ECB): Responsible for monetary policy for the eurozone. Based in Frankfurt, the ECB is run by an Executive Board. Its members and the governors of central banks in the eurozone comprise ECB's Governing Council. ECB and central banks together form the European System of Central Banks (ESCB), whose primary objective is to maintain price stability. None of these participants may take instructions from any other body.

European Coal and Steel Community (ECSC): Launched by the Schuman Declaration of 9 May 1950, placing coal and steel sectors of six states (Belgium, France, Germany, Italy, Luxembourg, Netherlands) under a system of common governance. The *European Economic Community* and *Euratom* were based on the ECSC's institutional structure. The treaty lapsed in 2002.

European Commission: See *Commission*.

European Community (EC): The EC is the central *pillar* of the *European Union*. Incorporating the *European Economic Community*, the *European Coal and Steel Community*, and *Euratom*, it contains federal elements of the *European Union* institutions and is responsible for the bulk of European Union activities.

European Convention on Human Rights and Fundamental Freedoms: A framework for the protection of human rights across Europe, adopted in 1950 by the Council of Europe. *European Union* states are all signatories and it is a basis for the respect of human rights in the European Union. The EU's Charter of Fundamental Rights is based in large part on the Convention.

European Council: Comprises the Prime Ministers of the member states, Presidents of Finland and France (who have some executive functions), and President of the *Commission*. Takes decisions that require resolution or impetus at that level and defines political guidelines for the *European Union*.

European Court of Justice (ECJ): See *Court of Justice*.

European Defence Community (EDC): A bold attempt in the early 1950s to integrate the armed forces of the *European Coal and Steel Community* states, shelved by the French National Assembly.

European Economic Community (EEC): Established in 1958 by the *Treaty of Rome*, its competences included the creation of a common market among the six member states and wide-ranging economic policy cooperation. Its main institutions were the *Commission, Council, European Parliament, Court of Justice*. It is the basis for today's *European Community*.

European legal order: The *Court of Justice* has established key principles of Community law. One is 'direct effect', enabling individuals to secure their rights under Community law in the same way as member states' laws. Another is 'primacy' of Community law, ensuring it is evenly applied throughout the Community.

European Monetary System (EMS): A precursor of *Economic and Monetary Union*, its key element was the Exchange Rate Mechanism, limiting exchange rate fluctuations.

European Parliament (EP): The directly elected body of the *European Union*, its *Members* (MEPs) have substantial powers over *legislation*, the *budget*, and the *Commission*.

European Political Cooperation (EPC): Intergovernmental foreign policy cooperation, introduced in 1970 and replaced in 1993 by the *Common Foreign and Security Policy*.

European System of Central Banks (ESCB): See *European Central Bank*.

European Union (EU): Created by the *Treaty on European Union*, with two new *pillars* alongside the central *Community* pillar, for cooperation in foreign and security policy and in 'justice and home affairs'. While the three pillars share common institutions, the two new ones are predominantly intergovernmental.

Federation: A federal polity is one in which the functions of government are divided between democratic institutions at two or more levels. The powers are usually divided according to the principle of *subsidiarity*, the member states or constituent parts having those powers that they can manage effectively.

Free movement: The treaties provide for free movement within the *European Union* of people, goods, capital, and services, known as 'the four freedoms'.

Intergovernmental Conference (IGC): The main way in which the *European Union*'s treaties are revised. Member states' representatives in the IGC draft an amending treaty, which must be ratified by each state before it enters into force.

Legislative procedures: Most *European Community* laws are enacted under the co-decision procedure, giving both *European Parliament* and *Council* powers to accept, amend, or reject legislation. The cooperation procedure, which gave the EP less power, is no longer important; but the consultation procedure, where EP is merely informed of Council's intentions, is still quite widely applicable. The assent procedure gives EP powers over accession treaties, association agreements, and some legislative matters.

Maastricht Treaty: See *Treaty on European Union*.

Members of the European Parliament (MEPs): Currently 785 MEPs are elected to the *European Parliament* from across the member states. MEPs represent their constituents; scrutinize legislation in committees; vote on laws and the budget; supervise the *Commission*; debate the range of *European Union* affairs.

Nice Treaty: See *Treaty of Nice*.

Non-compulsory expenditure (NCE): Expenditure over which the *European Parliament* has more power than the *Council*, currently around half the total *budget*.

North Atlantic Treaty Organization (Nato): Founded in 1949 as the security umbrella for Western Europe, tying in the US to the European security system.

Open method of coordination: An increasingly common means of getting member states to share information and best practices without the use of legislation.

Own resources: The tax revenue for the *budget of the European Union*. The main sources are percentages of member states' GNPs and of the base for value-added tax; smaller amounts come from external tariffs and agricultural import levies.

Permanent representations: Each member state has a permanent representation in Brussels, which is a centre for its interaction with the *European Union*. The head of the representation is the state's representative in Coreper (see *Council*).

Petersberg tasks: The military and security priorities for the EU's foreign policy. They include humanitarian and rescue tasks; peacekeeping; and crisis management.

PHARE: Assistance for the process of transformation in Central and Eastern Europe.

Pillars: The *Maastricht Treaty* set up the *European Union* using a pillar system. Each pillar is relatively autonomous, though linked to the other pillars by a set of common provisions. The central pillar is the *European Community* and the other two are for the *Common Foreign and Security Policy* and *Police and Judicial Cooperation in Criminal Matters* (originally known as *Cooperation in Justice and Home Affairs*).

Police and Judicial Cooperation in Criminal Matters: See *Cooperation in Justice and Home Affairs*.

Presidency: The *Council* and *European Council* are chaired by representatives of one of the member states, on a six-month rotating basis. The President-in-Office also heads the representation of the *European Union* under the *Common Foreign and Security Policy* and helps to set the direction of the EU for that period.

Primacy: See *European legal order*.

Qualified majority voting (QMV): See *voting*.

Regulation: A *European Community* legal act that is 'binding in its entirety and directly applicable' in all member states.

Schengen Agreements: Originating in 1985 outside the *European Union*, the Schengen Agreements now cover all member states save Ireland, the UK, and to some extent Denmark. The Agreements have been incorporated in the *European Community* (see *Area of Freedom, Security and Justice*).

Secondary legislation: Laws enacted by the institutions within the powers given them by the treaties.

Single European Act (SEA): Signed in 1986, the first major reform of the Rome Treaty. It provided for the 1992 programme to complete the single market; added some new competences; extended the use of qualified majority *voting*; enhanced the role of the *European Parliament*.

Structural funds: Cohesion Fund, Regional Development Fund, Social Fund (see *cohesion policy*).

Subsidiarity: A principle requiring action to be taken at *European Union* level only when it can be more effective than action by individual states.

TACIS (Technical Assistance to the Commonwealth of Independent States): Assistance for the process of transformation in CIS states.

Treaties of Rome: See *European Economic Community* and *European Atomic Energy Community*. The EEC Treaty is often called 'the Treaty of Rome'.

Treaty of Amsterdam: Signed in 1997, it extended the scope of co-decision and reformed the *pillars* on foreign policy and on justice and home affairs.

Treaty of Nice: Signed in 2001, the Nice Treaty provided for institutional reforms in anticipation of the enlargement to Central and Eastern Europe, with new voting weights and procedures, and more use for *enhanced cooperation* procedures.

Treaty on European Union (**TEU**): Signed in 1991 at Maastricht, it established the *European Union*. It laid down the procedures for creating *Economic and Monetary Union*; gave *European Parliament* important new powers; introduced a European *citizenship*; set up two new *pillars*, for *Common Foreign and Security Policy* and *Cooperation in Justice and Home Affairs*.

Union: See *European Union*.

Voting: most decisions are now taken by Qualified Majority Voting (QMV), which gives each state a number of votes, based approximately on its size. To pass, legislation requires 255 out of 345 votes, with the support of a majority of member states representing at least 62% of the EU's population. Unanimity applies less frequently to *Community* legislation but is prevalent in the other two *pillars*. Voting by simple majority is rare and mainly limited to procedural matters.

Western European Union (**WEU**): Created in 1954 by the UK and *European Community* member states. After a long period of inaction, the *Maastricht* and *Amsterdam* Treaties provided for links between the *European Union* and WEU, which is being incorporated into the EU and developed as a European arm of *Nato*. Most members of EU are members of WEU.

World Trade Organization (**WTO**): The 1995 successor to Gatt, WTO regulates international trade. It aims to reduce barriers to international trade and has mechanisms for resolving disputes.

Index

Page references in *italics* indicate
illustrations and their
captions.